# TYRANTS OF MATRIARCHY

Feminism and the Myth of Patriarchal Oppression

STEPHEN JAROSEK

ISBN 978-0-9775261-3-0

Published by Integral Cognito - 2<sup>nd</sup> edition (2021)

Grateful acknowledgement is given to the following for permission to quote from previously published material:

Excerpts from the ANGLOBITCH forum on The Ineffable Mystery of Anglo Hypergamy (October 3, 2012), copyright © edited by Rookh Kshatriya, reprinted by permission of Rookh Kshatriya.

Grateful acknowledgement is given for the cover image, *Weathered road leads into abandoned city*, copyright © Bruce Rolff (rolffimages/123RF Stock Photo).

Grateful acknowledgement is given to Paul Elam for his editorial services.

Because of the dynamic nature of the internet, any web addresses or links referenced in this book are subject to change by their respective authors, and may no longer be valid after this book's publication.

# CONTENTS

CONTENTS

# PREFACE

In the first edition of this book, published in 2013, a coherent model for the cognitive sciences had not materialized. Since then, much has changed. Donald Trump became president. And then former president. Trump Derangement Syndrome became a thing, and it became permissible to criticize feminists, as well as every other manifestation of far-left over-indulgence. Thus the workload for this second edition has been considerably reduced. There is less need to explain in detailed discourse, and it became necessary to trim the 2013 edition of all the verbiage.

Furthermore, in this revised edition, I take a closer look at the theoretical frameworks that can account for gender roles in culture. It is thus necessary to review the Darwinian paradigm, and more specifically, its neo-Darwinian incarnation.

Evolutionary psychology provides us with useful insights into human evolution, for example, in the context of sexual selection. But neo-Darwinism is ill-equipped to explain human nature and the gender roles with which we identify, within our cultures. I introduce an outline for an alternative theoretical framework in the first chapter.

The absence of a compelling theoretical framework, to properly account for gender roles in culture, provided feminists with the opportunity to insert their own oppression narrative. And in the absence of any serious challenge to it, feminism has gone on to become a dominant narrative of contemporary, progressive-liberal culture. In their solipsism, feminists believe that they've transcended patriarchal objectivism, but in reality, feminism is among objectivism's most toxic by-products.

The whole of feminist theory is built on an unsubstantiated premise. According to feminists, men have for millennia conspired in a misogynistic agenda to deny women fair treatment and to keep women "in their place." And from this myth, driven by the zeal of fanatics, was born the feminist lie of patriarchal oppression. That this lie could persist for the best part of half a century, to impact as it has on our lives, compels us to take stock.

The feminist-inspired mantra that women have been oppressed for millennia by The Patriarchy is pure fiction. No living system in nature comprised of two sexes can ever survive by privileging one sex to the exclusion of the other. Patriarchy does not emerge, on its own, from a vacuum. Matriarchal influences are especially important in first establishing in infants' rapidly developing minds the things that matter.

For humans, it is Woman as primary nurturer, who first defines the things that matter. Hers is "the hand that rocks the cradle," she is the Queen Bee around which all cultural purpose revolves. She has primary access to young minds, and so she has the greatest opportunity to establish the things that matter in young, developing brains. It is under Woman's watch that an infant first intercepts the experiences that begin wiring the neuroplastic brain.

Matriarchy as Queen Bee is everywhere in nature and everywhere in culture. It doesn't matter what culture we are talking about or what religion characterizes its values, from Islam, Judaism or Christianity, to Buddhism, Taoism or Hinduism.

Matriarchy operates behind the scenes. She is like the lion tamer controlling a formidable beast. We are amazed when we see this dangerous beast submit to the lion tamer's chair-and-whip, but we forget that it was raised among humans from the time it was a young cub. The trainer gets away with their act because they have first dibs at defining the things that matter in the young cub's mind. And this is precisely the same principle that the primary nurturer also employs in order to inculcate young, malleable minds into her culture's norms. It is always the primary nurturer that "defines the things that matter" and it is in accordance with the "things that matter" that young, impressionable neuroplastic brains are wired.

Every culture comprises both matriarchal and patriarchal dimensions without exception. Talking about a culture as if only the patriarchal exists in the absence of the matriarchal is the height of ignorance. It is feminists who render matriarchy invisible. Feminism is the ultimate conspiracy theory replete with all the delusion, denial and self-loathing that we can expect of the grandest among conspiracy theories.

# CHAPTER 1

# THEORETICAL OUTLINE

The semiotic theory of American philosopher Charles Sanders Peirce, in synthesis with the biosemiotic theory of Estonian biologist Jakob von Uexküll, provides the theoretical framework on which this book is based. In Jarosek (2013)[1], I outline how gender roles can be understood from the perspective of a few axiomatic principles, namely:

1) Gender roles are habits;
2) Gender roles are chosen;
3) Men and women *like* the roles to which they have been assigned;
4) Imitation plays a central role in how men and women acquire their gender roles.

This is a framework that connects the psychology of men and women, inextricably with culture. It is culture that provides the options from which men and women choose. This introduces a crucial shift in understanding, because *it is experiences from within culture, not genes, that have the greater impact on how the brain wires itself.*

This is an approach that provides as decisive a blow against feminism as any. Indeed, its impact is more compelling than that provided by the Darwinian paradigm, because it provides an account of matriarchy that has greater agency, and therefore greater responsibility for everything that is good and bad in culture.

## The limitations of Darwinism

Darwinism has played an important role in our theory of biology, and it is still relevant today, within the context of evolution and natural selection. However, some concerns with Darwinism remain... for example:

- Darwinism accounts for some important principles in biology, but it does not provide a complete, self-consistent framework for the life sciences in the way that Isaac Newton provided for the physics that bears his name;
- Gregor Mendel's research on inheritance provided answers to questions that Darwin had puzzled over, regarding the mechanisms of heredity. Clearly, genetics is important in the life sciences, but there are nuances that neo-Darwinism had failed to properly address;
- Neo-Darwinism, with its obsessive, genocentric[*] determinism, relies on assumptions about mutations and genetic causation that are inconsistent with entropy (the tendency to disorder). It is therefore necessary to draw a clear distinction between Darwinism and neo-Darwinism;

In simplest terms, neo-Darwinism is not equipped to provide the sorts of inferences that I make throughout this book. It provides no explanation of cause-and-effect, beyond the deterministic assertion attributing first cause to selfish genes, natural selection, and the DNA blueprint.

Neo-Darwinism fails to provide any coherent answers with respect to motivations, who is in control, who is oppressing whom, who is responsible for what. It sheds no light on how meaning evolves in culture and language. Neo-Darwinism sets the stage for conjectures and disputes that can never be resolved. This creates an intellectual vacuum that feminists have been able to exploit, thus

---

[*] Defined in glossary.

enabling them to get away with making all sorts of unsubstantiated conjectures and assertions.

Feminists might disagree with the substance of the patriarchal, deterministic theory that is neo-Darwinism (together with the original Darwin), but feminism could never have attained its level of influence in culture without it.

# THE MIND-BODY PROBLEM

The mainstream life sciences have been frustrated by the mind-body problem, with its dualistic assumption of mind as distinct from body. This is the essence of Cartesian dualism, which was addressed by Rene Descartes in the 17th century. It is a problem that persists to this day, impacting on all our mainstream cultural narratives, from information technology and artificial intelligence to Darwinism and, especially, neo-Darwinism. Indeed, the neo-Darwinian narrative of bottom-up determinism is perhaps *the* classic manifestation of the mind-body problem.

People working in artificial intelligence often entertain the idea of achieving immortality by downloading someone's personality onto a computer hard drive. Again, this is a typical manifestation of the mind-body problem that continues to badger researchers in IT and robotics. It is a fiction that will never be achieved, because the body is not a separate entity to mind. Minds can be *simulated*. But they cannot be manufactured. Robots and neural nets are *simulations* that do not experience anything. *Experience* and the attribution of *meaning* is the crucial difference.

## The body wires the neuroplastic brain

More precisely, it is experiences intercepted by the body that wire the neuroplastic brain.

It was Norman Doidge, M.D. (2008)[2], who pioneered the idea that experiences wire the neuroplastic brain. The body provides the interface between experience and mind. It therefore follows that how the brain is wired is contingent on the body that intercepts experiences. The brain of a human with hands and vocal chords is wired differently to the brain of a dog with four paws and fur. The neuroplastic brain of a man is wired differently to the neuroplastic brain of a woman, by virtue not only of their physiological differences, but also the choices that they make from culture. Bodies play a fundamental role in how reality is intercepted and perceived, because bodies provide the tools with which we make choices.

Maslow's famous aphorism is often bandied about as an anecdotal motherhood statement, without appreciating its full relevance to the mind-body problem. But it is very significant, and it deserves to be emphasized here:

*To a man with a hammer, everything looks like a nail.*

We can reframe this important insight in the context of sex and gender roles:

*A human whose only tool is a man's body will perceive the world differently from a human whose only tool is a woman's body.*

This tool metaphor, comparing the body to a tool-kit that wires the neuroplastic brain into its functional specializations, provides much more compelling explanations for the behavior of the many different kinds of animals that exist. There is no such thing as instinct, programmed into the brain, directing how a creature should behave. You can never explain mathematics to a dog because it hasn't the body to apprehend why mathematics should matter. Without vocal chords or hands, a creature with four paws and fur is not equipped to engage with culture in the same way that humans do.

It is said that dolphins have a brain-body weight ratio comparable to that of humans. If it were possible to transplant an infant human brain (before functional specializations have consolidated) into an infant dolphin body, and have it adapt, develop and function normally without fear of the brain being rejected, then that dolphin does not transform into a water-bound human; it does not become a "smarter" dolphin. We can reframe the mind-body problem, more generally, as follows: A dolphin (or dog or bird or fish) behaves as I would behave if I had the body of a dolphin (or dog or bird or fish). This is key, because the dolphin's new neuroplastic brain establishes its functional specializations through the experiences intercepted by the dolphin's body, exactly as it did before the transplant operation (presuming, of course, that the dolphin survives this thought experiment). It is essential to understand this unity between mind and body, in order to overcome the Cartesian dualism that persistently dogs the Occidental paradigm.

We might prefer to replace the tool metaphor, as the means by which we act upon the world, with the window metaphor, as the means by which we see the world. A body, as the window through which the mind sees and senses the world, will render invisible the things that lie beyond its field of view.

Whether as tool or window, the body is the platform on which the mind engages the world. Mice are not equipped to see the things that eagles see; and vice versa. The neuroplastic brains of both wire themselves to accommodate the experiences intercepted by their respective bodies.

Neural plasticity is an integral part of the mind-body dynamic, and the relationship between the choices we make and how our brains are wired. My article (2013)[3] was my original contribution towards unraveling the relationship between mind and body.

With the correct interpretation, the mind-body problem vanishes. It shouldn't be the mystery that it presents to our life sciences, even with their narratives trapped in neo-Darwinian determinism and the computer metaphors of IT. We can only conclude that they're too heavily invested in an ill-fitting paradigm that has far exceeded its use-by date.

It is beyond the scope of this book to go into further detail on the mind-body problem. However, it is of special significance to gender roles and how men and women relate to one another, and so a cursory introduction, at the very least, is obligatory.

# GENDER ROLES IN CULTURE: THREE LEGS OF A TRIPOD

The neo-Darwinian paradigm, with its emphasis on genetic causation, is a bottom-up interpretation that fails to recognize the importance of top-down causation originating from outside the organism. Culture, by contrast, displaces the need to rely on genetics to explain behavior. It is culture that informs humans how to behave, not genes.

Engaging with the cultural known is accomplished, principally, from three perspectives:

1) Entry and assimilation into the cultural known;
2) Exploring the unknown that lies beyond culture;
3) Immersion within the cultural known and identification with culture.

# 1st leg – Matriarchy, gateway into the cultural known

*Matriarchy defines what matters in the cultural known.*

In contrast to the Darwinian paradigm, the semiotic paradigm (the theory of language, symbols and meaning) is better placed to recognize a fundamental relationship between experience and how the neuroplastic brain is wired. And for most people, their first encounter with experience is most likely to have been through their primary nurturer. And in cultures the world over, it is the mother to whom the primary nurturer role defaults. For most people, it is their mother who first introduces them to how the world should be interpreted. "World" relates to culture.

The mother is everybody's primary trainer, training them about the ways of their culture and the things that matter within their culture. Once we accept the mother's role in defining how culture should be interpreted and prioritized, it should be self-evident that the mother's role is far from trivial.

The mother introduces her newborn into her culture. The first sounds that the infant hears, the first sensations it feels, the first images that it sees, revolve around the mother's voice, touch and presence. Her voice, touch and presence provide the initial conditions of a trajectory that begins at birth. She stands at the gateway into the cultural known. Her whole psychology and biology prioritizes the cultural known. She inculcates into her child the cultural values that they are expected to prioritize. It has been estimated that 90% of the wiring within a child's brain takes place within the first four years of life. By the time that a child reaches maturity, their mother has had far and away more than enough time to influence the neuroplastic programming that shapes her child's destiny. From the *initial conditions*[*] at birth, until the child's initiation into adulthood, the mother's influence over the neuroplastic wiring that takes place in most every human brain is far-reaching.

It is the matriarchy as primary nurturer that first establishes "the things that matter" in the mind of the child… the child that grows into adulthood to do their part in perpetuating culture.

For humans in culture, matriarchy is the first leg of the tripod.

## 2nd leg - Patriarchy at the exit from the cultural known

*Patriarchy questions what matters in the cultural known.*

Patriarchy's station at the exit from the cultural known and into the unknown contends with possibilities that have yet to be discovered and forms that have yet to be imagined. These relate to epistemology and ontology. From our cultural known we acquire our assumptions (habits). From the unknown beyond culture arrive the insights that transform, and provide the basis for new assumptions and new ways of being. These contend with matters of spirituality. At the interface between culture and the unknown beyond culture, a man's priority is to test possibilities. He must confront truths. He has to better himself in order to be able to confront the elements that challenge him, and to compete with others who oppose him. His interpretation of the world is constantly being tested, and he must rise to the challenge in order to survive. The father competes at work to provide, he fights in wars to defend, and he will die, if he must, defending what he values.

Evolution, cultural evolution, developments in science, any progress of any kind, emerges from the interface between the cultural known and the unknown that lies beyond.

Initiation ceremonies, in different cultures, are directed at introducing young boys entering adulthood, into the manly roles that their cultures prioritize. In this contemporary era, dominated by the leftist/feminist narrative, it can be difficult to identify what the

---

[*] Initial conditions, within the narrative of dynamics sytems theory, relate to the seed values that impact critically on the future developmental trajectory of the system. *Ref* glossary.

man's role should be. We can look to the animal kingdom for clues. The male lion as the king of his pride, the bull elephant in his solitary majesty, the silverback gorilla and his leadership on which his troop rely, the male lyrebird and his enchanting mimicry of sounds from the forest... the animal kingdom provides us with many clues to inform us what the male role might be.

The father, as a role model, stands at the gateway that exits from the cultural known. He is about possibilities, about growth, and what a child might become, within their lifespan, before their turn arrives to exit from their cultural known.

For us humans, spirituality is first and foremost a masculine enterprise, because it contends with the unknown in ways that the matriarchy never can. It is how we evolved from the stone age to the Renaissance, science and the arts.

However, the masculine-spiritual role is not one that is cast in stone. There are also examples in the animal kingdom where the male role can be anything other than spiritual. Hyenas are matriarchal and with their pseudo-penises, these matriarchs are authoritarian bullies. Their male counterparts are smaller than the female, and their skulking body-language gives them away as supplicating submissives to the authoritarian matriarchs of the clan.

Likewise, the angler fish flips the script with regards to matriarchal and patriarchal roles. In hyenas and angler-fish, there are examples where human gender roles might go when the male supplicates to female authority. And it is often not a pretty sight.

For humans in culture, however, patriarchy is the second leg of the tripod.

# 3<sup>rd</sup> leg - The cultural known

*Culture, identity, and knowing how to be within the known.*

The third leg of the tripod is culture. Culture impacts on identity and perception of self. Culture provides the basis for how we know how to be. How a person negotiates their options, across their parents and culture, determines what they become. Should either (or both) parent(s) fall down on their responsibilities, there is always the third leg of culture to immerse oneself in, to work out one's own path through the incredibly complex maze that is reality.

The three legs of the tripod… matriarchy, patriarchy and culture… form the basis for our reality. They account for the human psychological profiles that constitute our cultural norms, and the stereotypes that deviate from them.

## Neo-Darwinism fail

From this brief outline, it follows that Darwinism, in both its original and its neo incarnations, provides little explanatory power for sex and gender roles. How could it? A narrative relying on concepts such as *instinct* and *adaptive traits*, stands little chance of apprehending how organisms interpret their worlds, and give meaning to them.

The original interpretation, however, as framed by Charles Darwin, provided some important insights and principles for the life sciences. Darwin was not a neo, because he could not have been. He had not heard of the work of his near-contemporary, Gregor Mendel, who lived far away in another country, spoke another language, at a time when news and letters depended on delivery by Pony Express. The theory of genetic inheritance had not caught on at that time. Darwin is fairly widely, if controversially, considered to have been a Lamarckian[*]. And so, I reserve my greater criticism for the neo-Darwinian interpretation.

Within the neo-Darwinian narrative, it is materialism (mechanistic physics and math) that projects its linear, deterministic assumptions. The male lyrebird's astonishing ability to mimic the sounds of the forest is not for the sheer joy of creation, but because, according to neo-Darwinists, it is an adaptive trait that is sexually selected by the female lyrebird, to enable both their genes to propagate into the next generation. Likewise, within the neo-Darwinian narrative, the leadership and authority of the silverback gorilla in his troop has nothing to do with courage and earning his place at the top of the hierarchy, and everything to do with dominance as an adaptive trait that is sexually selected by the female

---

[*] In Lamarckism, or Lamarckian adaptation, an organism acquires characteristics through use or disuse throughout its life, and passes on these characteristics to its offspring. The classic example of Lamarckism that is often cited in the literature is the giraffe's long neck.

gorilla. And both get to propagate their genes into the next generation.

The majesty of animals in the wild, their dramas, their familial loyalties and the bonds between friends, their struggles for survival, and the motivations of all living things are dismissed with the bland sterility of instinct, "adaptive traits", genetic causation and selfish genes. The neo-Darwinian interpretation fails in the life sciences, and so why should it be taken seriously in the human social sciences? It is sterile; dead in the water. A semiotic narrative is far more compelling and descriptive. It is from the perspective of the semiotic narrative that this book proceeds, to provide an alternative analysis of gender and the culture wars.

# THE GAMETE MODEL
# OF SOCIAL ENGAGEMENT

The social dynamic that plays out between men and women in culture, is analogous to the sperm-egg dynamic that plays out at the level of the gamete. The egg is the object of desire, and of the multiple sperm that try to gain access, only one sperm ever gets lucky. Let's give this dynamic a name, and call it the gamete model (of social engagement).

The gamete model of social engagement describes gender roles in culture. The receptive ovum need do nothing other than choose. The onus is on the sperm to do everything. A man can be the most successful, best looking, most charismatic guy in the world. Women might gravitate around him like bees around a honey-pot. But if he does not embrace his inner sperm and initiate any action, he won't get the girl.

The gamete model opens the way for an alternative explanation for the gay phenomenon. Men who don't embrace their inner sperm won't figure out what all the fuss about women is, and so they won't be motivated to initiate anything. Men must learn their responsibility, as sperm, and act on it. Most men learn early in life, about their responsibility to "man up". For most men, this comes easily enough, through the cultural narratives in which they immerse themselves, and the assumptions that they incorporate. Traditions, custom and language, along with markets, prostitution and pornography, play an integral part in reminding men of their needs, and indoctrinating men into their role as sperm. Men are *hard-wired* with "needs" (goes their inner dialogue). Men that embrace the cues from culture will have no problem doing the performing monkey routine, and women will have no problem accepting it as "just" how men are. And among the men who fail to embrace their inner sperm, some might believe the answer to their disinterest lies in their inner gay... they are not "wired" as other men are (goes the inner narrative).

Men who are disinclined to accept their cultural cues, regardless of how interesting they might be to women, are said to start out life behind the eight-ball. Are they losers and failures? Are they gay? Or is there, indeed, something that is undignified about being required to perform like a circus monkey, begging for treats, to prove oneself a worthy provider?

In order to be successful with women, a man has to jump through many hoops. The first most essential hoop is, of course, embracing his inner sperm, and accepting the indoctrination to which culture expects him to conform. Other hoops, depending on how one defines "success" with women, include social proof, and working on those social displays that indicate a "well-adjusted," good provider. And to impress those ladies that conflate thug and degenerate with dominant and exciting, mumbling while you make like an emotionally stunted adolescent can pay dividends.

A young buck getting a driving license and a car while still in high school can often provide an edge over more serious, plodding types that want to work on their qualifications and careers first. Having a car to drive is not just a status symbol. It's a provider symbol. A car is not just a guy thing. It's a provider thing. A youth with a car doesn't even need to be conscious of its significance. He just needs to pursue what he's passionate about, and he learns it first from the choices he makes from culture - perhaps while he's still in high school, reading car magazines and collecting memorabilia of his favorite sports heroes.

When a young man gets his Game right and he initiates, the young, single woman's "yes" is a foregone conclusion. Or at least he assumes as much, and most of the time he will be right. That odd occasion that he's wrong is a part of the thrill of the chase, and he embraces it with his love of risk. Should he hesitate, deliberate or supplicate, then nine times out of ten she will spook and he won't see her for dust. She won't be able to get away from him fast enough.

The gamete model of social engagement explains why the techniques of Game can assist men in the dating market. Women naturally predispose as incels[*], in the sense that if dating were left to the initiative of women, nothing would ever get accomplished. Psychologically, from the perspective of agency and locus of control, women are little different to incels. Indeed, Coach Red Pill (2020)[4] suggests that the key to success with women is to treat them like nerds; the overlap between incel and nerd is not misplaced. This is why men can benefit from knowing about Game. It teaches them that women think very differently to men, requiring a fundamental shift in frame from that which a man maintains with his buddies.

The gamete model of social engagement provides the basis for a frame where she yearns to connect with a greater whole to which he belongs; a domain in which he is in charge. [In a sense, we might interpret feminism in precisely such a context – feminists have been trying to seize the domain of men, without understanding the risks, responsibilities and commitments that are required within it]

Our gamete model explains the proclivity of many women, these days, to monkey branch across relationships. Instead of having to confront solitude on her own, a woman can pave the way for a new relationship even as she maintains an existing, perhaps unsatisfactory relationship. Whether her existing relationship is growing stale or she's a narcissist who's open to exploring better options (fobo – fear of better options), there is often no shortage of beta orbiters[†] for a woman to choose from. Or if there is, it is not difficult for her to find new possibilities, from among the many spermatozoa that comprise her social circles, to encourage and nurture.

I suspect that within the incel community are many men who've grown up without a strong father figure to guide them. In the absence of strong male role models in their lives, they've not been taught to embrace their inner sperm, and they must invariably turn to their mothers for insights into how the world should be interpreted. Under Mother's dominating influence, they can never overcome the first hurdle that blocks sperm from access to ova; they

---

[*] Defined in glossary.
[†] Defined in glossary.

never learn the importance of taking the initiative. Women will never yield to men who are confined to the female manner of engaging with women. Women don't want more conversation, more touchy-feely empathizing and emoting; for that they have their girlfriends. By definition, a woman *cannot* yield to him who does not take.

This brings us to an interesting question. If a woman likes a guy but he declines from taking the initiative, why doesn't she just do something about it? The answer is very simple. She can't. As the ovum, taking the initiative is way beyond her comfort zone, requiring her to assimilate conflicting narratives, both internal and external (cultural), that are cognitively dissonant with how she understands gender roles should play out. And for her to take the initiative is to factor in an even greater risk that he won't be able to assimilate her breaking the rules. The accepted cultural template makes things easier for everyone, when everyone knows what the rules are.

## The priorities of men and women in a nutshell

With our new interpretation, we are better placed to interpret men's and women's different priorities. It now makes sense why security and relationships are the priority of women, and freedom and adventure are the priority of men. The gamete model of social engagement provides a far more reliable and consistent explanation for gender roles than any of the other explanations that have done the rounds thus far throughout human history.

# CHAPTER 2

# IN THE SERVICE OF CULTURE'S QUEEN BEE

## 2.1 BRAIN IN A VAT

In this somewhat tongue-in-cheek analysis, I examine the difference in intelligence between men and women. The normal bell curve distribution is often addressed metaphorically to describe women's distribution in parameters like intelligence as being taller and narrower, while that of men's is flatter and wider. Essentially the point being that men occupy a wider variation on parameters like intelligence, from incredibly dumb to incredibly smart, while women occupy a comfy medium. There is less variation in performance and abilities among women than there is among men. It turns out that on average, the intelligence of men and women is the same.

This is all well and good, except that there is another dynamic playing out in gender differences. There is something called *sexual dimorphism* (Wikipedia - Sexual dimorphism, 2012)[1]. This is a term from the mainstream biological sciences where the male and female evolve to acquire different phenotypic traits[*]. In the case of

---

[*] These are the observable physical or biochemical characteristics of an organism, as determined by both genetic makeup and environmental influences.

intelligence, there are grounds to infer that provided-for women who never have to do anything except shop, dance and nurture, lose their intellectual capabilities. In their provided-for lives without moral responsibility, their brains atrophy. To appreciate why this should be so, it is necessary to dump the mainstream *evolutionary psychology* (EP) paradigm grounded in *genocentrism* (defined in glossary).

## Habits of indulgence

Men and women value attractiveness in women. Especially within the Anglosphere, a woman's entire worth is established almost exclusively on her physical appearance and how she packages it. The EP crowd have an explanation for the importance of female beauty. They will blather on about attractiveness as being an indicator of health, superior genes, etc. Meanwhile, the *Game* and *PUA* (Pickup Artist) community[*] worship beautiful women at the Altar of Gynocentrism, and women who can package themselves to look attractive enjoy privileges and entitlements that are not extended to those women who either fail to pay attention to their packaging, or for whom no amount of packaging can salvage.

But there is one dimension of womanly existence that is never taken seriously, especially within our current zeitgeist, and that is a woman's intelligence. Personality may rate to some extent; her readiness to laugh at men's jokes, her social savvy, her ability to get drunk just like men do, her ability conform to the expectations of her peers, etc. But these are aspects more related to groupthink rather than those deeper qualities that we associate with intelligence; such as curiosity, integrity, skill, commonsense, courage, etc. This raises a most important question. Can the disconnect between beauty and brains ever be reconciled? In terms of universal possibilities, I'm confident that it can, but in terms of human life on Earth and our current trajectory, the answer is no, it cannot. Trying to reconcile the beauty-brains disconnect within the context of our zeitgeist and culture is a fool's errand.

---

[*] *Game* and *PUA* (pick-up artist) are references originally taken from the controversial seduction community... refer to glossary.

# Atrophy of the mind

It is well established now that PUAs, as performing seals begging for fish, routinely work themselves into a lather about what women think of them, and then construct elaborate strategies to demonstrate to their *objet de l'amour* that they don't care what women think of them. And the extent to which women's opinions matter is proportional to where these women rate on the attractiveness scale. The unspoken rule is that the opinions of nines and tens are weighted more than the opinions of fives and sixes, while the opinions of ones and twos are weighted probably nothing at all. There is no rational reason for this instinctive association between attractiveness and credibility. It's a subconscious reflex, a bias.

This manner of thinking comes about because of the EP paradigm and the genocentrism on which it is based. Women who are deemed to be attractive are valued more, and so Game theory extends the fantasy by rationalizing that they must also be "better" at other things, such as intelligence and calculus. And these "higher quality" women demonstrate their intelligence in their social savvy. This is naught but projection, receiving its inspiration from a culture obsessed with female beauty and then attributing to it various assumptions that are unfounded.

Let's take a closer look. What if the reverse is actually true? What if intelligence is more likely to be *inversely* proportional to attractiveness? There is sound reason to expect this to be the more likely truth. There are various theoretical frameworks available to suggest this, whether they are grounded in religion, customs, psychology, semiotics or science, for example, and within many of these frameworks is the idea that habits play a crucial role in character formation. In the first instance, there is the semiotic theory of Charles Sanders Peirce, whom I reference in Jarosek (2013). But other references include Quote Garden (2010)[2], Green (2007)[3], Wikipedia – Charles Sanders Peirce (2012)[4], and APRU (2009)[5].

Sometimes these habits might be described in terms of "units of imitation," and this relates to the field of memetics and the spread of memes (Wikipedia - Memetics, 2012)[6].

Where do these habits, or memes, come from? The answer is, culture. The provided-for sex has permission to be, well, provided for. These days, a woman has permission to work (if she wants) or to do nothing (if her fancy takes her). Affirmative action grants her freebies and entitlements to which men have no comparable access. And of course, the prettier that a woman is, the more privileges and entitlements she can indulge in. For all her practical utility, she might as well be a brain in a vat.

Traditionally, women's stay-at-home option was a part of the marriage contract, a division of labor that came with responsibilities, from raising and schooling children to domestic and social duties. Implicit within this contract was moral conduct. Sharing the load with her husband, these environmental pressures and the attendant division of labor between the sexes constantly tested everyone at the boundaries between self, family and environment. So, imagine how intelligent... not... today's prettiest stay-at-home must be, given that she no longer bears the onus of these responsibilities. Today's provided-for stay-at-home must be the ultimate hippopotamus wallowing in freebies for which she does not have to account. She is a parasite sucking the lifeblood from her clod provider and as useless as a brain in a vat. A brain in a vat is not sustainable – without stimulation from the environment, it is destined to turn to mush.

Now, it is true that women often derive considerable stimulation from texting, gossiping, shopping and dancing. However, these forms of stimulation are not comparable to things like fixing a car, creating a computer, composing a work of art, or working out a business strategy. So, what do we notice here in the differences in the ways in which men and women think? In women, it's the absence of decision-making. There is no outcome to decide on in the process of texting, gossiping, shopping or dancing, beyond consolidating popularity with your girlfriends or simply, pure indulgence for its own sake. And while housework and shopping for the family have an important part to play in domestic responsibilities, decision-making is rarely as consequential for women as it is for men. There are limited risks in deciding on one brand of hairspray over another. For women, there are no consequences for mistakes that are comparable to getting sand in your engine, or misaligning the head of your engine, or messing up a masterpiece, or creating a short circuit on a circuit board, or your opponent getting wind of your strategy. Men must make things work... often to the extent that it can become a matter of life and death. For women, texting, gossiping, shopping and dancing are not quite as dangerous or risky. Many things that women do can be done in their pajamas, without even having to venture beyond the front door. Women's activities may stimulate memory and white matter (glia), but they won't stimulate the grey matter… the neurons.

And here we come up against an essential property of all living things. Namely, a mind that is never tested is a mind that atrophies. Use it or lose it, as the saying goes. It applies as much to men as it does to women. It's just that men's role as a utility device limits their options for being an unproductive parasite. There is evidence that the "use it or lose it" principle is pervasive throughout the animal kingdom.

## Sexual dimorphism in the anglerfish

Feminists will be delighted to read of the apparent role reversal between the male and the female anglerfish - refer The Oatmeal (How the male angler fish gets completely screwed)[7] and Wikipedia - Anglerfish (2012)[8]. The female anglerfish is everything that the you-go-grrrl crowd could hope for. She is the embodiment of what feminists imagine men to be, but with female body-parts. She's a feminist dream come true. She patrols the ocean as an independent, free spirit, hunting for her food, using the fleshy lure dangling in front of her mouth to attract food. She is the provider, maintaining her modest harem of clingy males in the lifestyle to which they have become accustomed. The differentiated sex roles of the anglerfish is an example of *sexual dimorphism* (Wikipedia - Sexual dimorphism, 2012).

It wouldn't be quite accurate, though, to think of her harem of clingy anglerfish dudes as castrated. Rather, quite the opposite – it's not their testicles that disappear, but their body. Their testicles become the most important aspects of their being. Their only value appears to be in becoming testicles. If we recall Germaine Greer's famous quip describing women as life-support systems for wombs, well, the poor male anglerfish's mind and body amount to nothing more than a homing device for testicles. Once this homing device for testicles has accomplished its goal – which is to pair up with a female (much like a PUA) – the rest of his being atrophies. His brain, his digestive organs, liver, eyes – everything but his testicles – basically, "poof"… vanishes.

27

The reason that the human PUA does not atrophy as completely as the male anglerfish, however, is that though his intelligence, honor and integrity are compromised in his reliance on validation from women, he is a utility device who still has to provide for himself. His somewhat diminished existence continues to be tested in the workplace. His productivity would be rather limited if all that remained of him was a pair of testicles. As disappointing as the PUA is as a human being, his usefulness as a utility device will exact demands of him that will always test his existence at his boundaries. In the case of the male anglerfish, by contrast, no comparable demands are placed on his survival, because he is fully provided for in the nutrients that he receives from his provider host – his entire identity is thus destined to atrophy, though his testicles will remain. The male anglerfish, in contrast to the male human, *can* sustain his existence as a pair of testicles, once he has found true love in anglerfish heaven.

So, what can we make of this, in terms of understanding the nature of human intelligence? The nature of intelligence has always been a source of controversy. How do we measure it? I won't attempt to answer this question in the course of this chapter. However, we can infer some appreciation of the nature of intelligence by considering the behavioral trajectory of the male and female anglerfish.

The male anglerfish, for all intents and purposes, ceases to exist once his testicles, attached to the female anglerfish, become the last remaining vestige of his being. The female, by contrast, maintains a robust identity, with her body and brain fully developed. With the fleshy lure attached to the end of her elongated dorsal spine, which she dangles in front of her mouth to lure prey, she is able to provide for herself. As a provider, her conceptualizations of reality are constantly being tested, and so she maintains a fully functioning mind-body that does not atrophy. Furthermore, not only is she able to fend for herself, but she is also able to provide for her harem of clingy males (up to six at a time), who draw their sustenance from her body at the point at which they first attached themselves, back when their minds and bodies were intact as homing devices for testicles (before they became mere testicles).

What lessons do we take away with us from the anglerfish? Firstly, we need to incorporate a systems view of life - refer

Wikipedia – Systems theory (2012)[9] and Panarchy.org (2012)[10] and the idea that living entities self-organize in order to accommodate the choices they make (this contrasts with the evolutionary-psychology perspective that presumes that everything is accounted for in the genetic blueprint). In this context, the human brain rewires itself to accommodate the choices that a person makes - refer to Doidge (2008)[11] and Wikipedia – Gerald Edelman (2012)[12], and the idea that the brain is a kind of ecosystem comprised of neurons. Provided we accept the systems view, then the following reasoning makes perfect sense:

- Any living entity whose existence is not tested at its boundary atrophies. While aspects of this atrophy can be noticed over its lifetime, if the absence of environmental stimuli persists over the generations for all members of the species, then the atrophy becomes especially important to its evolutionary trajectory. If an entity's muscles are not tested, they become flabby. If its eyes are not tested, then, over the generations, they disappear. And of course, if its conceptualizations are not tested, its synaptic connections degenerate, and its brain atrophies, both within its lifetime, and over the generations. Systems theory resonates with aspects of Lamarckism;

- The gender that provides is constantly having its conceptualizations of reality tested at the boundary. Well-defined physical strength, mental agility, resourcefulness, agency, are resources that are essential to making decisions at the boundary (in this context, "boundary" refers to the point of equilibrium between organisational structure and environmental pressures – an organism is only as muscular or intelligent as it needs to be in order to ensure its survival);

- The gender that is provided for also has its conceptualizations tested at the boundary, but because being provided for imposes fewer demands, atrophy in comparison to the provider is inevitable... unless an alternative stressor is introduced to test the provided-for's boundaries;

- The stressor that has tested women's boundaries, for the best part of human history, has been the matriarchal, primary nurturer role. It is only in the contemporary, post-feminist,

29

contraceptive-dependent, abortion-on-demand culture that that stressor has been virtually eliminated.

## Bottom line

Intelligence might be difficult to define, especially given the current state of our life sciences. But the end points of a trajectory can be established with some amount of certainty. The mature male anglerfish, at the end-point of his provided-for trajectory, for all intents and purposes has no brain. By inference, the mature female human, at the end-point of her provided-for trajectory and in the absence of historically traditional stressors, should have an atrophied brain in comparison to the male. The only way that the human female can avert neural atrophy is by moral conduct, because it is only in moral conduct that her conceptualizations can be tested at any boundary that is comparable to that of the male. It is only in moral conduct that she can realize that there is a price to be paid for indulging in freebies that are not earned... or for making stupid lifestyle choices.

# 2.2 INVISIBLE OPPRESSED WOMEN

## The patriarchal oppression that never was

We know how the spiel of "nice feminists" goes... women were oppressed for millennia by The Patriarchy, and we needed feminism to put a stop to the oppression of women. Nice, "reasonable" feminists often point out that The Patriarchy also hurts men, and by challenging The Patriarchy, feminism also benefits men. They might sometimes even acknowledge that perhaps feminism has gone a bit far and that some kind of "correction" is called for... but, by and large, in the grander scheme of things, they will continue to parrot that feminism is a cause for good.

All well and good, except for one small problem... feminism never ever had a legitimate claim. There never was any such thing as a unilateral, one-way oppression of women by men, and to buy into such an absurd thesis is to fundamentally fail to understand how cultures and people's minds work. By blaming some mythological unilateral patriarchal oppression that never was, they render invisible the matriarchal oppression that defines the things that matter. In their obsession with the purported invisibility of women, they render women... invisible.

There is an alternative paradigm, however, one that establishes that every living organism takes its cues for behavior from its ecosystem... and for humans, that ecosystem is culture. Experience wires the neuroplastic brain (Doidge, 2008)[13] and for humans, that experience is cultural.

## Matriarchy's primary nurturer

It is almost paradoxical that in obsessing about the invisibility of women, feminists have served to make women even more invisible by discounting the area in which women's influence is most potent... their role as primary nurturer. For it is in their role as primary nurturer that they first impress upon their children *the things that matter*. This applies irrespective of which culture or religion we are talking about. From Christians, Muslims and Hindus, to Buddhists, Pacific Islanders and Kalahari bushmen, those with first dibs at defining the things that matter in the minds of their children are the culture's primary nurturers, who generally tend to be women. Women's expectations and priorities are generally impressed upon their offspring from infancy through to early childhood, and these first impressions wire the brain most profoundly. It is only in later years, from later childhood and on their transition into manhood, that boys are encouraged to break from their maternal comforts, apron-strings and security and "patriarchal" influences begin to dominate. Before reaching this stage, the foundations for neural wiring have pretty much been laid, and the young man is most likely to have his mother to thank for his initiation into "the things that matter." The things that matter... these are the assumptions – the "given" that we take for granted – that most every person takes with them from their infancies and childhoods into adulthoods and old age. This interpretation is fundamentally at odds with the mainstream, genocentric paradigm.

When children first learn about the things that matter, they learn about power differentials, about getting attention and getting along, and whether they behave with kindness and civility or selfishness and hostility. These dynamics are first impressed in children while their brains are most absorbent as sponges for experience.

The relationship between single-mother households and criminality is well established (Facts on Fatherless Kids)[14]. It is also well established that women are the primary abusers of children (Administration for Children & Families, 2002)[15]. Single motherhood and child abuse are two of the ways in which toxic mothers define the things that matter. Children first learn violence from their primary nurturer.

The bottom line is this, and it is a most important point. Oppression within cultures is never unilateral, never one party to blame. Culture is a whole, a complex system where everyone, in their cultural narrative of shared assumptions, is somehow complicit. And in trotting out the Patriarchy shibboleth, feminists manage to deflect attention away from the reality of women's very real contributions to crime and violence.

## Defining the things that matter

What do I mean by "defining the things that matter"? What I am getting at is a principle from philosophy defined as pragmatism (Wikipedia - Pragmatism, 2013)[16], and quite beyond the purpose of this book, as it goes into the existential/phenomenological questions relating to how an entity defines "the things that matter." The essential point must, however, be made. It is the primary nurturer that first establishes the cultural/social transactions and their terms that have the greatest bearing on the wiring up of the brain of the infant/child under their care. When we factor in the relevance of neural plasticity and how the brain develops, it is clear that stimulation from the environment is essential to healthy brain development (Shatz, 1992)[17]. The infant enters the world with approximately 2,500 synapses per neuron, by age three that number grows to 15,000 synapses and by adulthood the number of synapses per neuron is culled to about half that number (Cherry, What Is Brain Plasticity?)[18]. Life experiences are crucial to how the brain wires itself. There are critical periods for the developing child wherein if certain skills have not been acquired by a certain age, it is unlikely that the individual will ever acquire that skill. For example, according to the critical period hypothesis, if language is not acquired within the first few years of life, attempts to acquire a language beyond the critical period (some time between 5 years and puberty) become much more difficult and less successful.

The primary nurturer is primary caretaker, primary guardian, primary teacher, during the most crucial, formative years of a child's life when the brain's development is at its most dynamic. And it is in these formative years that the primary nurturer's role in defining the things that matter is so important. Child abuse and its transactions matter, and stand a high probability of being translated into anti-social conduct in the mature adult.

Stefan Molyneux recognizes the urgent implications of child abuse with respect to adult health and social problems (Molyneux, 2009)[19]... and also that women are the primary abusers of children (Molyneux, 2013)[20]. In his discussion of the biology of violence (2009)[21], for example, Molyneux observes that:

> During the first 4 years of life, 90% of a child's brain develops *through the experiences* of that child.

This widely-repeated claim is perhaps best substantiated in the work of Dr Jill Stamm of Arizona State University: (Stamm, 2007)[22], (Stamm & Spencer, 2007)[23] and (cbresearch, 2007)[24].

During the first 4 years of life, it is reasonable to conclude that the primary nurturer will have the greatest impact on defining the things that matter, and this will impact profoundly on how the child's brain is wired. This will ultimately have the most potent influence on the adult that that child becomes. In traditional two-parent households, the father's role is to intervene and provide a corrective to motherly influences. In single-mother households, by contrast, the mother's world-view proceeds unrestrained, its reflexive, solipsistic impulsiveness is allowed free reign without being tested, and this sets the stage for unrestrained, impulsive delinquency in the child.

# The schizophrenogenic mother

Before feminism came onto the scene, the notion of the schizophrenogenic mother was widely accepted as playing an important part in the genesis of schizophrenia in patients. In view of the intimate relationship that the mother has with her child during that period of its life when brain development is at its most dynamic, this should not be surprising. If it is the mother that first defines the things that matter for the child, then it is not unreasonable to factor in the relationship between the role of the mother and the schizophrenia that might develop in her child later on. The typical profile of a schizophrenogenic mother suggests that she is cold and authoritarian, inclined to withhold love, or maybe provide love on conditional terms in which guilt plays a central role.

In her analysis of patterns of behavior profiled by criminologists of perpetrators who imprison and sexually abuse their victims (with particular reference to Josef Fritzl, Viktor Mokhov, Aleksandr Komin and Wolfgang Priklopil), Galina Sapozhnikova (2008)[25] observes that the perpetrators all had authoritarian mothers:

> Surprisingly, Fritzl, Mokhov, Priklopil and Komin are similar in both history and profession. They were all crazy about their mothers, grew up without fathers and were beaten in childhood. All their mothers were strong women. Fritzl's mother kicked her husband out and Mokhov's mother controlled who Mokhov brought home in the evenings even when he was 53. Priklopil was also close to his mother.

Among the worst of these profiles, that of Josef Fritzl, references to his abusive mother are well documented. Writing for the Guardian, Kate Connolly (2009)[26] reports on what the forensic psychiatrist assigned to Fritzl had to say:

> ... Kastner said his behaviour had its roots in his troubled childhood, describing a mother who did not love him, who left him to cry when he was in pain, and who regularly beat him and left him on his own for hours at a time.

In view of the incarceration by the authorities of the aforementioned perpetrators, it would seem that they may not have quite qualified as schizophrenic... the parallels are clearly evident, though, and the differences between them are probably academic.

More specific to the topic of schizophrenia, Scott Peck writes, "I frequently found the mothers of schizophrenics to be extraordinarily narcissistic individuals" (Peck, 1978)[27].

Theodore Lidz was an American psychiatrist who was famous for his books and articles on the causes of schizophrenia. From Wikipedia (Wikipedia - Theodore Lidz, 2012)[28]:

> Lidz noted that schizophrenogenic mothers manage to be impervious to the needs and wishes of other family members. "As her psychotic or very strange concepts remain unchallenged by the husband, they create reality within the family". Dr. Lidz calls this phenomenon *folie à deux*, a shared delusion between two parents. And if the delusional ideas of the dominant parent are shared by all family members, the result is a *folie en famille*.

Of course, in these politically correct times, what suggestion that women might in any way be held accountable for their actions should not be accompanied by a disclaimer? Accordingly, Wikipedia cites Lidz criticising the culture of blame against schizophrenogenic mothers:

> I also find it very distressing that because the parents' attitudes and interactions are important determinants of schizophrenic disorders, some therapists and family caseworkers treat parents as villains who have ruined the lives of their patients.

Anne Harrington's (2012)[29] article, however, is more in keeping with the spirit of our time:

> The psychiatric profession is appalled by the burden and pain that was once inflicted by telling families, and especially mothers, that they had literally driven their children crazy.

Is it sexist to suggest that mothers are more likely to have a crucial part to play in the genesis of schizophrenia? Is it wrong to pick on mothers for bad mothering practices? If it is, then why is it perfectly acceptable to continue with the myth that all men are inherently violent and need to be "educated" to not rape? Bad mothering in all its permutations is, after all, the flip side of violent or criminal or dysfunctional behavior. Of course, nothing of this is to exempt men from responsibility for their own behavior, but equally importantly, you cannot consider violence – or schizophrenia - in the absence of the role of the primary nurturer. General consensus has it that thus far throughout most of human history, that role has been ascribed to the female of the species.

## The exciting bad boys of women's choosing

To understand the choices that women make, we need to understand that men's and women's brains are wired very differently. It sheds some light on the matter if we realized that men have more grey matter (neurons) and women have more white matter (glia), and that these have a direct bearing on men's and women's conceptualizations of the world. It was found in intelligence tests (Haier, Jung, Yeo, Head, & Alkired, 2005)[30] that on average, men used 6.5 times as much grey matter as women, and that women used 9 times as much white matter as men. It's almost as if men and women were different organisms, quite literally. If we factor in neural plasticity and the idea that the brain wires itself with experience, then it is logical to infer that the reason for these differentials is that the provider sex and the provided-for sex make very different choices from their culture. Men's problem-solving, deliberative style of decision-making impacts more heavily on the wiring up of neurons, while women's consensus-motivated, relationship priorities impact more heavily on the wiring up of glia (white matter).

The outcome is as ridiculously simple as it is obvious. If you provide for someone, male or female, babying them throughout their lives, they will never grow up. In the contemporary climate of feminism where women are not required to take responsibility for their choices, culture sanctions the favoritism of women in spheres as diverse as law, employment, education and entertainment. The end result is spoiled, entitled women who have never had to compete on their own merits. This impacts on what they become, because they are denied the challenges that are so important in the cognitive development that depends on the wiring of brains.

In having concluded that men and women think very differently, it should also occur to us that men's and women's sexualities express themselves differently. These are the dynamics of desire and being desired, the pursuer and the pursued. It is beyond the scope of this book to go into this in detail, so we will need to take it on face value for the time being that there is a logical relationship between female sexuality, women's rape fantasies (Hutson, 2008)[31] and the contexts that they find arousing. More specifically, there would appear to be something about violence, or criminality, that women often find arousing. For example, Otto Weininger (1906)[32] famously observed the relationship between criminality and prostitution. Kevin Solway provides an online reference to Weininger (The main parts of Sex and Character, by Otto Weininger)[33]. It would not be too much of a stretch to interpret Weininger's references to prostitution within the context of our own zeitgeist's women and permissive culture. The relationship between the slut and the bad boy is the contemporary manifestation of the older, more "traditional" relationship between the prostitute and the criminal.

As one of the pioneers of the PUA (pick-up artist) movement, Chateau Heartiste (2012)[34] draws our attention to the reality that "chicks dig jerks." His interpretation is substantiated in the work of Kayt Sukel, who references a study where single women had their brains MRI-scanned as they looked at photos of men whose faces had been altered to appear more or less masculine. It was found that the subjects were most attracted to the masculinized faces – and that the regions of the brain that were activated indicated that these were the men that the subjects found most threatening (Sukel, 2012)[35]. This further substantiates our observation that dangerous men resonate at a visceral level with women's sexuality. Feminist women notice violent men over non-violent men because it gets their juices flowing... it is that subconscious stuff operating at a primal level that ties in with women's rape fantasies and lights up the threat centers of women's brains like a christmas tree. As Chateau Heartiste observes, "I'm fond of saying the boner doesn't lie. The same could be said of lit-up neurons; hard to fake that funk."

From among all the different kinds of men that exist... moral men, kind men, brave men, courageous men, thoughtful men, spiritual men, creative men... feminist women notice, first and foremost, violent, abusive or dominating men. Why is this? They are projecting how *they* see men, and what they value in men. When feminists claim that all men are rapists and oppressors, they are not describing a truth that applies to all men, but instead, revealing an inner narrative that sheds light on how they interpret the world and what they value within it.

## Conclusion

Women need to be held accountable for:

- How they raise their children;
- The choices they make in men.

Of course, men should continue to take responsibility for their own behavior as we've always done. But the idea that men alone are to be held responsible for violence is just another feminist lie.

With respect to violence in culture and the purported invisibility of women (according to feminists), the following should by now be self-evident:

- Children first learn violence from their primary nurturer;
- Men learn what women like in men from the types of men that women choose – it's the reason that PUAs learn Game.

The bottom line is, quite simply, that there is no such thing as The Patriarchy acting in a vacuum. There is a patriarchal-matriarchal duality, and women are equally responsible with men for all that is good and bad in culture.

# 2.3 THE CHOICES WOMEN MAKE

## Women's dopey choices – the practice

To properly understand matriarchal power we need to explore the dynamics of how power is exchanged between men and women. To this end, our sampling of narratives from the PUA/Game community goes some considerable way to illustrating our thesis.

Our analysis should not be taken as support for the methods of PUA Game; far from it.

> PREAMBLE: Before we venture further into this topic, perhaps here is a good point to pause, to establish some distinctions. We should distinguish between two broad categories of Game. On the one hand there is Game that a father might teach his son as he enters into manhood, about courage, his responsibilities as a man and his bearing in relation to women. And on the other hand there is Game as typically interpreted by the PUA community, modeling itself on the bad boy stereotypes of lad culture. The latter is less about individualism and integrity, and more about mimicking the methods that work with women. It taps into an adolescent narrative that harnesses tension; for example, in displays of dominance, or clever put-downs (negs). Between these two extremes are shades of grey. Game can indeed reveal insights to the uninitiated. For example, the importance of confidence, body language or social proof, might come as an epiphany to those young men who start out believing that women just want a nice, reliable provider to settle down with.

Ultimately the gynocentrism that provides the basis for PUAs' motivations is the same gynocentrism that we recognize in chivalry. Insofar as the adherents of PUA Game might claim some measure of success, their methods remain contingent on the pedestalization of women, in return for their dose of validation from women. As such, the PUA/Game narrative does nothing to restrain the feminist juggernaut... indeed, it exacerbates the problem by trapping men in the assumption that men have "needs" and women have the solution. Within the context of the PUA/Game narrative, the role of Man as circus animal, performing tricks for a biscuit and a pat on the head, is in lockstep with the tradition of Man as provider and all-round utility device. There are far worthier goals for men to pursue.

The following excerpts from a forum conversation were taken from Rookh Kshatriya's website Anglobitch (Kshatriya, 2012)[36] on the topic of *The ineffable mystery of Anglo hypergamy**. In the interest of relevance, I omit detailing the comments from other parties, other

---

* Definition of hypergamy in glossary.

than Kshatriya and myself (ToM, for Tyrants of Matriarchy). This conversation might come across, at first glance, as unconstrained conjecture, but it is invaluable because we are brainstorming interpretations that can shed light on how women perceive reality.

**ToM** 11 October 2012 00:00

> I do get what Rookh is saying, but I disagree with him that women go out of their way to always choose reprobates and degenerates. For one thing, many women do often choose dull but predictable providers (such as computer nerds, lawyers, doctors, auto mechanics, car salesmen, etc, etc). These plodding types are by no means comparable to mumbling thugs and degenerates, and it is not fair of Rookh to make that comparison. While it is true that to many women, a degenerate thug is way more exciting than an autistic accountant [ToM is an accountant btw, if anyone wanted to know], it is definitely not a given that a woman is going to choose a degenerate thug over an autistic accountant. An autistic accountant does, after all, have utility as a provider and that defines his purpose. This provider utility has value and is not to be so easily dismissed and brushed aside.
>
> The key to understanding women's choices is to understand that they are more inclined to accept their reality, their environment and its definitions. They are creatures of proximity - meaning, that they will enter into relations with whomsoever constitutes their proximity. It relates to their solipsism, and the idea that their environment is perceived as reality. As creatures of proximity, women too readily accept the environment and its terms. If they hang with losers, they will choose losers. If they hang with computer nerds, they will choose computer nerds. If they work as secretaries at the front desk, they'll choose from the sales reps and managers who hit on them, or whatever milieu exemplifies their work environment. If they chance upon a pimp, they might become prostitutes. If they chance upon a priest, they might become nuns. Men, by contrast, are more inclined to be

independent agents choosing their own proximity and thus, their destiny.

The bottom line is this. As creatures accepting their proximity, women are too easily removed from the dating market, and this creates a shortage in supply with an excess in demand. Men develop all these complex theories suggesting that women are picky, hypergamous alpha-choosers when the truth is much more likely to be the very opposite. In fact, it's the arbitrariness of women's choices, not their pickiness, that explains how and why women finish up with the men that they do.

> PREAMBLE: Anonymous (11 October 2012 08:21) objects to my comment "They [women] are creatures of proximity - meaning, that they will enter into relations with whomsoever constitutes their proximity." Anonymous' objection is based on the deeply flawed western assumption that ultimately men and women are both equally predisposed to choices based on proximity. This idea that like is inclined to pair up with like is an unrealistic, romantic notion that is easily dispensed with by referencing the dynamics of Game, in all its gory detail. The simple truth is that "nice" women are far too easily won over with a bit of Game and that cads do far too often get the gal, while their "nice-guy" beta equivalents are routinely banished to a barren wasteland devoid of love or validation. The harsh reality for nice-guy betas is that there is very little like pairing up with like. The idea of finding one's soul-mate, especially in our contemporary zeitgeist of hookup culture, is patently unsound. Yet this like-with-like fiction persists, nay thrives, in the minds of both men and women. "Nice guys" as betas, banished to the wastelands, continue to search for "true love" not realizing that they've missed the bus long ago while "nice girls," easily removed from the market, believe that they've found "true love" in some predictable monkey performing tricks in return for treats. I responded:

**ToM** 11 October 2012 19:26

No, it's not impossible at all. It works by changing the dynamics of pairing-up. If you think in terms of free-ranging, independent males pairing up with free-ranging, independent females, then you won't get it. Instead, the free-ranging, independent males (or patient beta orbiters who have learned to bide their time) typically find themselves pairing up with dependent, serial-monogamist females who are on the rebound. Women continue to be "monogamist" and they continue to be dependent. Hence the notion of serial monogamy, where women who are in the process of transitioning across relationships are typically caught on the rebound. In this model of serial monogamy, women might choose from fresh, uncharted territory, or they might fertilize future prospects who, as stable beta orbiters, strike when the opportunity avails itself. Because women don't understand men, choosing from uncharted territory (like going to a pub to meet PUAs and other assortments of strangers) is risky. It is usually safest for a woman to select from her ever-present bevy of beta orbiters.

**Rookh Kshatriya** 11 October 2012 07:23 responding to my post 11 October 2012 00:00

> *"For one thing, many women do often choose dull but predictable providers (such as computer nerds, lawyers, doctors, auto mechanics, car salesmen, etc, etc)"*

True, but that often occurs in their thirties and late twenties after spending their prime years chasing thugs and deadbeats. When they sense the biological clock ticking, they start looking for some solvent 'bore' to pick up the pieces of their ragged lives. The feminist hatred of this site hinges on the fact that it explains female motivations to all the 'bores', 'wimps' and 'losers' they once shunned - and it does so in telling detail.

**ToM** 11 October 2012 19:56

As per my reply to Anonymous immediately above, I disagree. You often find young women from traditional or religious traditions choosing from the dullest bores, often because of the promise that they might show as future providers. Usually, in conjunction with said signs of future promise, fertilized, well-nurtured proximity yields a woman the desired result. And if it all gets too hard and her plan goes awry, there is usually a bevy of ever-present beta orbiters to rescue her.

I think the key to understanding women's choices is proximity, and NOT independent self-determination. In other words, women's choices are more arbitrary than they are controlled or directed. It is true that women often engineer the proximity that they desire by manipulation, but in view of women's materialistic priorities and/or what they define as sexy in men (e.g., the mumbling bad-boy), these manipulations usually run their course with ridiculous outcomes.

**Rookh Kshatriya** 11 October 2012 21:30

It is often said (and I doubt it not) that middle class women attend elite colleges not to study but to snag rich husbands. That would be an example of women seeking out environments congenial to their hypergamous aims rather than merely accepting the environment they grew up in. In fact, women are also now more likely to go to college in the Anglosphere than men. I think working class women still accept their environment and adapt to it - but that goes for working class males as well.

One of my pet ideas about female mate-selection being arbitrary and dysfunctional is that it has undergone little evolutionary refinement. That is, female mate-choice exerted little influence for most of human evolutionary history - all that was taken care of by 'soft rape' (sexual coercion of women via formal institutions such as arranged marriages) and 'hard rape' (direct sexual coercion in the aftermath of war or conquest). Consequently, female mate-selection (a relatively new concept) has far greater plasticity (and is far more prone to dysfunction) than its male counterpart. So, in the 80s women were attracted to girlish men because the media told them to be; now, it tells them to like thugs and criminals, so they like thugs and criminals. As men, we find this malleability hard to grasp - male sexuality has evolved logically to prefer youth, thinness, large breasts and symmetrical features. Female sexuality is far less 'logical', largely because it was never subject to rigorous evolutionary competition. And this applies to women in general: because they are mostly 'guaranteed' the right to reproduce (whatever their personal qualities), they are generally retrograde in mental and physical terms. For example, 70% of photosensitive epileptics are women; women have lower average IQ; women are more superstitious; and so on.

**ToM** 12 October 2012 02:58

Seems like we're on the same page. Though our interpretations could do with a bit of refinement. Women are drawn to the formidable (respectable) in man. However, the formidable presents something of a quandary. Almost by definition, the formidable spooks women... it is intimidating, and this sets her rationalization hamster into overdrive. "Oh he noticed my blemish" "Oh can he smell the garlic on my breath?" "Oh he thought I meant x when I meant y" "Oh is he mad at me now?" "Oh he's noticed my small tits." Solution? The ideal compromise for a woman is to choose that version of formidable which has eliminated the spook factor. Enter mumbling degenerate, stage left.

She chooses an idiot, one that combines the best of both worlds - excitement without the spook factor. He is threatening, yet not threatening. He is threatening because as a degenerate thug there's an obvious element of danger about him, yet because he is dense and insensitive, he's easy to read and predict. Most importantly, as an insensitive brute, he does not expect much of her, and so she won't feel so self-conscious, like she's under the spotlight. See how it works? If you are a woman, you can combine threatening with predictable by choosing a mumbling idiot slumped at a bar... and through such an astute choice, you get the danger without that constant nagging feeling that maybe he expects more from you. You get the excitement without the boooooring. And as an added bonus, you have the government handouts to fall back on in the event that you should birth his spawn. But you've got to make a choice... exciting thug or reliable provider? What's it to be girl? Quick, decide. Tradeoff. Do it. Submit, before he gets away.

**Rookh Kshatriya** 12 October 2012 07:27

If women's education were that significant, how come they still earn less? Besides, women generally shun 'difficult' subjects requiring mathematics or formal logic and prefer pointless degrees in subjects like art, English and sociology.

And another thing - men drop out and 'fail' (educationally if not economically) because Anglo-American women dislike any sign of intelligence in boys/men. If a guy wants a girl-friend he has to 'play the game' and pander to the reflexive female preference for thugs and morons. The alternative is found in the life of James Holmes: he followed the 'intellectual' path and experienced only involuntary celibacy for his pains. It doesn't take much smarts to see that dysfunctional female mate-preference is the primary cause of male educational failure in the Anglosphere.

**ToM** 12 October 2012 23:56

Rookh, I agree with you that women often go to university in order to score a husband. An ex of mine used to joke about that. She mocked Arts as Marriage 1 and Law School as Marriage 2. But I digress. A compelling anecdote does not a study make.

However, I do disagree with one aspect of your interpretation. Women do indeed choose sub-par men. But it's not because they go out of their way to choose degenerate, ugly men. Far from it. Who would go out of their way to choose that which is inferior, the worst of the crop? If you had a pick of 10 grades of apple in front of you, why would you choose the worst?

No, here's the reason to explain women's choices. Because women are, at a primal level, inspired by the formidable (respectable) in man, they feel intimidated by that which they most desire (as I explained previously). This situation predisposes women to self-esteem issues. Women are fundamentally uncomfortable in relating to formidable men. That's why it is so important for men to be able to disarm women, to make them laugh, have a sense of humor. THAT's the reason women choose degenerates. A degenerate is an optimum choice that provides a substitute for the formidable that a woman can never relate to. That's why many women relate most comfortably to those men who retain their adolescent immaturity... you know, the shallow, paper-alpha routine. It's the reason why Game can often work so well... it harnesses women's low self esteem. It's also the reason why many women choose ineffectual bores of the beta persuasion, where Game could actually jeopardize your chances (It's also the reason why feminism tries to level men, tries to make men look ridiculous, but I digress, that's stuff for another time).

Alles ist Klar, nein?

The end result is, of course, that women still make ridiculous choices, but women do NOT go out of their way to choose the fuglies. They don't say to themselves, "ewww, there's an ugly creep, I hope he hits on me." That's patent nonsense. Quite simply, women feel most comfortable, least threatened, by average men that blend with the furniture.

**Rookh Kshatriya** 13 October 2012 04:58

> *"Who would go out of their way to choose that which is inferior, the worst of the crop? If you had a pick of 10 grades of apple in front of you, why would you choose the worst?"*

This is the crux of the matter. While there is much truth in what you say, one important factor is that female sexuality, having a much higher level of plasticity (and therefore biological dysfunction) than male sexuality, is far less rational and effective in its instinctive decision-making. And this is explained by the 'soft' and 'hard' rape that have shaped human development for millennia. Because female mate-choice was obviated by power, money and war, it never evolved with the same purposive clarity as male sexuality did. This explains why men all over the world prefer youth, thinness, a slim waist and other physical signs of reproductive fitness. All attempts by feminists to make men prefer fat, old women have fallen on stony ground (thank God). Men in China, Sweden and the Amazon all want the same things, basically. You seem to be saying that female sexuality is much more shaped by social/psychological concerns, and this interpretation fits my general thesis quite well - sex, in short, is much more tangential to their sexuality.

While your psychological insights have much value, the psychological cannot be separated from the socio-cultural. And in the Anglosphere, women are told from earliest childhood that they are princesses in waiting. This, as we know, is an expression of the puritanical repression that forms a distinctive backdrop to Anglo culture. Many regular posters here (especially Americans) suggest that this 'pedestalization' creates a uniquely entitled outlook among Anglo-American women, especially the few attractive ones. One expression of this is the notion that 'no man is good enough', leading to spinsterhood on the one hand or thug-fucking on the other. All this is supported by the cultural exclusivity of dysfunctional female mate-preference - it is not nearly so strong outside the Anglosphere, despite continental Europe having far more generous Welfare programs.

However, your own points about the female fear of formidable men suggest that Anglo women - knowing themselves at heart to be inferior - are by nature ill-at-ease with their 'exalted' status. In itself, this doubtless contributes to their obsession with useless deadbeats. The higher they fly the harder they fall, and all that.

**ToM** 13 October 2012 20:03

Ah yes, I definitely agree with you there. The socio-cultural aspect is very important. This is what I refer to in the context of women choosing TYPES of men. The men that women choose have to stand for something. They have to have a label attached, make a statement. If a woman prioritizes being provided for, then that label will usually be a success marker, usually defined in terms of a man's career... like CEO, lawyer, doctor, soldier, etc. If a woman prioritizes fashion statements and fitting in, then the label that she will notice might be "pack leader," "degenerate thug," "party animal," or "reprobate layabout." The wonderful thing about the plasticity of women's sexuality is that they can actually get off on ugly men. But remember the first rule of type. It's not enough to be just a naked blobfish. The ugly man has to have a label. A limping, overweight midget with attitude, on his own, is not always a sure thing. But he can increase his odds by becoming a leader of a pack and sporting a patch over one eye... see what he's doing? He acquires agency over his label. And he can increase his odds even further by becoming a celebrity... e.g., the Hunchback of Notre Dame... then bingo, his odds skyrocket. And if he gets himself kitted out with sunglasses, a leather jacket and a limping swagger, he acquires an alpha distinction that sets him apart. Quasimodo the Hunchback of Notre Dame becomes Quasimodo the lothario legend. Women love celebrity... and by definition, the celebrity is the label.

The plasticity of women's sexuality is integral to how culture works. It enables ridiculous stereotypes to become reality, and this alleviates God's boredom, providing him with centuries of entertainment and amusement. He must be laughing his arse off, seeing the most charismatic, genetically gifted dudes competing against genetic throwbacks.

PREAMBLE: Eric (12 October 2012 00:08) reframes the previous objection made by that of Anonymous (11 October 2012 08:21 – see above). He wants to understand how proximity relates to women's preference for bad-boys who are not interested in monogamous relationships, and who nonetheless finish up with "more female attention than they can reasonably handle." He provides the example of "a rather unintelligent-looking guy, not at all handsome, and chronically unemployed," who fathered 30 children by 11 different women, all who knew of his reputation and thought of him as a legend.

One of the common themes running through these objections is that "nice guys," not used to intruding on a woman's personal space, never get to realize how easy it is to score with women - provided that a few simple rules of Game are observed. By contrast, women live with the assumption that "all men are only ever after one thing," and "everyone is doing it." And when some performing monkey with some rudimentary application of Game hits on them, many women, not used to the idea that the vast majority of men are actually quite restrained, succumb with minimal resistance.

An analogous dynamic of ignorance applies to the celebrities pursued by women. 4,000 women being serviced by 1 Mick Jagger (Von Glinow, 2012)[37] is not the same as 4,000 men being serviced by, say, an averaged mean of 200 women. Each one of those 4,000 solipsistic, hypergamous women is not tangibly conscious of the other 3,999 that she is "competing" against (though she may be aware of them in a theoretical kind of way, in an unmaterialized abstract). A woman's solipsism, for all intents and purposes, enables her to indulge in her fantasy that she might be The One that wins his heart – but either way, win or lose, it doesn't really matter to her because one alpha stud is worth a thousand supplicating betas.

The dominant reigning alpha absolutely can finish up with the lion's share of women, while the vast majority of his conquests are content to keep their numbers in the single or maybe double digits. And in the meantime, nobody need be aware of how imbalanced the tallies across men and women are. Both men and women are living with the same illusion that the numbers at least roughly pan out, and neither have any way of telling how wide of the mark their assumptions actually are. I responded:

**ToM** 12 October 2012 02:32

Eric, no contradiction at all. Regarding the assumption, post sexual revolution, that everyone is doing "it" (having sex)... How correct is this assumption? Who are the ones most likely to make this assumption, and who are the ones who are going to try to put it into practice? What do men assume to hold true about this assumption and what do women assume? How many alphas/ degenerates "service" a majority of the "nice girls"? How many sluts and/or prostitutes service a majority of the men? Who knows? The averages that pan out across men and women may surprise you... and maybe even me. The thing is that none of us has the complete picture. The question is, who's servicing whom and by what numbers? The only thing that I can suggest with any amount of certainty is that it is wrong to assume that men and women are going for it one-on-one. In this light, no, there need be no contradiction at all.

**Rookh Kshatriya** 13 October 2012 05:15

I like your term 'paper alpha' - something like an adolescent court jester. Women prefer that kind of tiresome monkey - agreed. Where Game goes wrong is in calling that kind of impish turd an 'alpha'. Genuine badass alpha dudes like Richard Kuklinsky in the States or Charles Bronson in Britain are not in the least attractive to women. If Anglo-American Gamers stopped confusing court jesters with genuine alphas, I'd have a lot more time for them. In fact, I would suggest genuine alphas have never evolved much Game, as a psychological type - historically, alphas have never had to 'court' women. They used soft (cultural) and hard (physical) rape to perpetuate their genes.

# More on women's dopey choices – the theory

## The power of projection

The differences in the ways in which men and women think call for a different strategy in interpreting and understanding our opposite sex. We should never take women's logic literally. We should learn to read between the lines. For example, if a woman tells you that she does not like something, do not always assume that she does not like that thing. You've got to read between the lines to understand why she notices that thing, what it is about that thing that relates to her experience of it, and so on. In other words, what is the context behind her dislike? Oftentimes shock and disgust over something (such as is typical in women's emotive reactions to rape) betray a fascination with that thing that is reflected in their fantasies, the choices that they make, or some other inadvertent manifestation of their innermost impulses. For example, shock and disgust with rape stories can actually project a fascination with rape and an inclination to fantasize about rape.

And when feminists accuse men of taking advantage of their positions of authority to oppress others, they are projecting. They are telling us what *they* would be doing if they were put in the same positions of authority.

And when feminists complain that it's not fair that only men occupy the most powerful positions of authority, they are projecting. They are telling us that men in power are the only ones that matter. Those men at the lowest ranks working as janitors, laborers and factory hands, don't matter. They're invisible. They don't count.

Let's illustrate the importance of projection with some more arbitrary examples. Consider the following quotations taken from A Voice for Men (Factory, 2011)[38]:

*Robin Morgan - former president of the National Organization for Women (NOW) and editor of MS magazine:*

> I feel that 'man-hating' is an honorable and viable political act, that the oppressed have a right to class-hatred against the class that is oppressing them.

*Former Congresswoman Barbara Jordan:*

> I believe that women have a capacity for understanding and compassion which man structurally does not have, does not have it because he cannot have it. He's just incapable of it.

*Catherine MacKinnon:*

> All sex, even consensual sex between a married couple, is an act of violence perpetrated against a woman.

*Marilyn French; The Woman's Room:*

> My feelings about men are the result of my experience. I have little sympathy for them. Like a Jew just released from Dachau, I watch the handsome young Nazi soldier fall writhing to the ground with a bullet in his stomach and I look briefly and walk on. I don't even need to shrug. I simply don't care. What he was, as a person, I mean, what his shames and yearnings were, simply don't matter.

Each of these women is projecting. Compare what they are saying, with your own experiences.

Robin Morgan is telling us that she is a vindictive, hate-filled person. By contrast, many of us have met men who are capable of taking on an opponent respectfully, impartially and in the spirit of competition, without vindictiveness or hatred.

Barbara Jordan is telling us what she notices and values in men. Cold, arrogant and unfeeling is hot, baby. By contrast, many of us have met many men who are caring and compassionate.

Catherine MacKinnon is letting her rape fantasies get ahead of her. 'Nuff said. On the odd occasion, she even borders on graphic:

> I think that sexual desire in women, at least in this culture, is socially constructed as that by which we come to want our own self-annihilation. That is, our subordination is eroticized in and as female; in fact, we get off on it to a degree, if nowhere near as much as men do. This is our stake in this system that is not in our interest, our stake in this system that is killing us.

Mmmm... sounds like the basis for a yummy rape fantasy.

And, saving the best for last, what is it that gets Marilyn French aroused? Well, nothing less than a "handsome young Nazi soldier." What is Marilyn French *really* telling us about her true values and what she expects of men? "My feelings about men are the result of my experience." Indeed. Here she is admitting to the very choices that she has made in men, and her inadvertent candor provides a welcome change.

The reality is that whenever we open our mouths, irrespective of whether we are men or women, we project something of what we value, what we notice. But there's a key difference between men and women as to what can be inferred from the projection. Men focus on the "external" (career, hobbies, interests), while women focus on the "internal" (me, me, me, I, me, I want, I need, I hurt). Projection of a passion for motor sports is thus not quite as insightful as the projection of spiteful contempt.

## Origins of feminism and sexism

Even the word *sexism* did not enter our vocabulary until feminists invented it, with its first appearance in a student-faculty forum in 1965 (Shapiro, 1985)[39]. So clearly, the least that we can infer is that there was something about the way that feminists saw the world that required inventing a new *-ism* for it. That is to say, where normal men and women defined gender differences and accepted their respective gender roles without complaint, feminists were always the original sexists because it was they who introduced the hate and envy that defined their movement.

In the context of gender differences and the concomitant division of labor in the workplace, there was always room to address questions of equal opportunity in the interests of fairness and maximizing human potential. It was feminism, however, that projected its own toxic self-loathing, interpreting this mostly innocent dimension of tradition as a conspiracy and thus providing the basis to fuel its own hate-driven agenda.

Therefore, feminism is more accurately described as feminists' projections of their own sexism.

# Women's dopey choices – the cure

## It's the culture, stoopid

As I've outlined in the first chapter, the paradigm that I implement to understand human sexuality and gender roles is very different than the established narrative of neo-Darwinism. This is particularly relevant in the following outline.

As discussed previously, the social dynamic that plays out between men and women is analogous to the sperm-egg dynamic that plays out at the level of the gamete. The egg is the object of desire, and of the multiple sperm that try to gain access, only one can ever win her heart.

It isn't generally obvious to men that women routinely make ignorant choices. The gamete model of social engagement explains why. Women are in control of the supply of sex, so men find themselves in the position of having to work out access to it. When men agree to women's terms, they enter the transaction validating its legitimacy, and also validating women's power. This blinds men to women's true nature. Perceiving women to hold the sexual power, men can only project their assumptions, as men, about power… they conclude that women know what they're doing. But the truth is that women don't know what they're doing. They are driven by assumptions based on personal experiences, not truths based on impartial observations. None of this is determined in the genes.

Women learn what men are like, first from their fathers. As they venture beyond family, they continue to learn what men are like from their culture; from the men that they work with, from the orbiters that vie for their attention, or from the types of men that hit on them. How a woman perceives men is contingent on the types of men to whom she gives airtime. She will never learn about other kinds of men, from men who make no attempt to engage her. It's the culture that teaches her, and never the genes that program her. Her behavior, her thoughts and her choices are not determined in her genes. These are determined exogenously, from the choices and engagements that she habituates and in which she immerses herself. These are determined in the culture that surrounds her.*

---

* A similar line of reasoning also applies to men… but within the context of the gamete model of social engagement. Men also learn about women first from their mothers, and

When feminists tell us how awful men are, they are, of course, projecting. They are telling us about the men that women notice, the men that matter to women. If a woman hates men, then she is projecting truths about how she's engaged with men in her past, and the kinds of men that she's chosen to engage with. Her experiences are the basis for her assumptions. If she's experienced a loving, responsible father growing up, then that will predispose her to predictably sensible kinds of choices she makes as an adult. If she's experienced an irresponsible, abusive father, then that will form the basis for her initial assumptions about men, and it will predispose her to predictable choices as an adult.[*]

The bottom line is this. When women hate men, it can never be based on objective facts. It can only ever be based on subjective experiences and previous choices. What does a woman's hatred of men tell you about the choices that she's made in her past?

## Women do not want to be your friend

One of the implications of the gamete model of social engagement in contemporary, western-feminist culture is that the most attractive women are being approached by men all the time. Because we've rejected the neo-Darwinian myth that men's and women's behavior is set in the genetic code, it makes sense that women's neuroplastic brains are wired by this relentless attention from men. And it is in this context that their conditioning is better understood. Men approaching women shapes how women think (and men approaching women, of course, shapes how men think). Women don't want to be every orbiting beta's friend. They want to be the King's lover.

If a man is not the King, the Boss, the Exceptional, if he hasn't the charisma to catch a woman's attention, or if he is not already among her family, friends and providers, then he is invisible, a mere fleck of lint on her Armani jacket. At best, he might be useful; a handy device, like a toaster or refrigerator. She might be momentarily entertained, she might play along for a laugh, a dare, or

---

beyond family, from their culture. But with the crucial difference that men are the providers, desirers and pursuers, while women are the provided-for, desired and pursued. But I digress.

[*] Ultimately, of course, an analogous interpretation applies also to men, because men's behavior must also take place in the context of experiences in family and culture.

maybe to see what use she can make of him. And she knows what men want; she learned this as an egg fending off sperm. And when she's extracted what *she* wants, she'll toss him aside like a used tampon.

Women are not interested in working alongside you towards your success. They'd rather wait at the finishing line and pick off the winners from there.

The gamete model of social engagement has important implications for gender roles in culture. Security is the birthright of women. Freedom is the birthright of men. Both have their rewards and penalties. How men and women actualize their birthrights provides the basis for their respective moralities.

**Further evidence for women's dumb choices**

The most compelling evidence for women's choices comes from them every time they open their mouths. They tell us. Every time that a woman tells us how awful men are, how it's difficult to find a decent man, how she hates men, she is projecting. She is telling us something about the choices she's made, and the culture she's immersed herself in.

Again, none of this is determined in the genes. It is established in the choices and engagements in which she's immersed herself, in her culture. To live in culture is to be conditioned by it. It is a kind of hypnosis. Culture is a hallucination. Culture is constantly reminding us what matters, who and what we are, and who and what we should be. What goes around comes around.

If women's behavior is not programmed into their genetic code, then where does it come from? What explains women's often outrageous behavior? Validation from men plays a central role. A woman will do astonishingly degrading things if she has a male audience urging her on. Her appreciative male audience urging her on is rewiring her brain to think that her degradation is no big deal, and she laughs it off. She is addicted to attention from men, and the male gaze. Why stop your fun when everyone's hollering and hooting for more? The losers with which she surrounds herself are the losers hypnotizing her to experience no shame. If women of 50 years ago were easily shamed for trivial breaches of cultural norms, today's women have flipped the script entirely and done a complete

180. None of this is in the genes. It is in the men they choose and the company they keep. It's the culture that they identify with.

It's that gamete model of social engagement, again. The egg wields enormous power over the many sperm trying to access her. But she too, is trapped, because she is addicted to the attention. She craves the attention like an addict craves crack.

And consider how, these days, women often seem to go out of their way to make themselves look unattractive. I refer to the before and after photographs of women that frequently do the rounds on the internet.

Before being influenced by feminism, she is wholesome, trim and healthy, cheerful, without pretense. After feminism, she's become bloated and unrecognizable, her scowl matching her edgy, dyed hairstyle, piercings, tattoos and goth-inspired lipstick and makeup. Where does that come from, if not the genes? It comes, again, from the men that they choose, the men that they surround themselves with. You don't need women to tell you about the kinds of men that they've been with. Their appearance can tell you what you need to know. A woman's appearance will tell you when she's been owned by degenerates. An integral part of human behavior in culture is imitation. Women who have chosen degenerates will dress in imitation of degenerates.

And here we arrive at the cure to our ignorance, with the simplest, most self-evident of our truths about women. Women who hate men do so because they choose awful men.

# CHAPTER 3

# MATRIARCHAL OPPRESSION IN CULTURE

There is little doubt that men are more prone to direct, active violence than women. There are other forms of violence, however, other characteristics that provide rich, fertile soil in which a violent outlook can develop. For example, there is the now well-established link between single mother households and crime (Baskerville, 1999)[1]:

> Recent figures from the Department of Health and Human Services confirm that violent crime, drug and alcohol abuse, teenage pregnancy, emotional and behavioral disorders, teen suicide, poor school performance and truancy all correlate more strongly to fatherless homes than to any other single factor, surpassing both poverty and race. The overwhelming majority of prisoners, juvenile detention inmates, high school dropouts, pregnant teenagers, adolescent murderers, and rapists all come from fatherless homes.

There is a very simple reason why women are less inclined to direct violence than men. The provided-for sex is obviated from the need to confront the bluntest truths that routinely wire the provider's brain. The provided-for sex is less likely to have to compete, confront or assert than does the provider sex. The provided-for sex reverts to relational aggression because they can. And relational aggression provides its own expressions of hostility, manipulation and ill-will that can ultimately manifest in violence. In this chapter I explore in more detail women's contribution to violence.

# 3.1 MATRIARCHAL AUTHORITY'S BASIS

## Relational aggression

Men and women are predisposed to different forms of aggression. In general terms, it is assumed that men favor direct or overt aggression, and women favor indirect aggression. These are generalizations, however, and there is no justification in assuming that one form of aggression is the sole preserve of either sex. Women can be overtly aggressive to their children, for example, often abusively so. And men often engage in indirect aggression themselves. Our emphasis here is on the psychology of indirect (relational) aggression, women's predisposition to it, and its impact on the female psyche.

Overt aggression is the kind of direct aggression that is "in-your-face," and is typically associated with direct verbal confrontation and physical assault.

Indirect aggression is "under the radar" aggression. And relational aggression is the term used to describe the kind of indirect aggression whose purpose is to harm a target's social status and relationships. As a form of indirect aggression, relational aggression is typically covert and behind-the-scenes, and is not intended to confront or resolve situations. Plausible deniability resonates with this kind of aggression. Given its covert nature, the purpose of relational aggression is usually destructive, since any discussion of conflicting interests, or attempt to arrive at their resolution, is avoided – that is, until the agony of trying to avoid one another becomes so unbearable that a truce has to be called.

The purpose of direct or overt aggression, on the other hand, is not always destructive. Often, the intention is to address problems or disagreements and to arrive at a mutually satisfactory solution.

Women, who prioritize networks, family and relationships, are naturally inclined to relational aggression. In the spirit of projection, they know that the things that they value, will be valued by others. And so they know how to apply relational tactics to hurt others. Gossip, exclusion, and manipulation are among the tactics favored in relational aggression.

Relational aggression constitutes part of an inner narrative that values social approval and fitting in with social networks. And so it is much more than just a strategy. It constitutes a pattern of thinking that confines one's behavior to acceptable norms. Conformity and groupthink are a part of that pattern. The locus of control, in relational aggression, is therefore external.

In direct/overt aggression, social approval is secondary to addressing and maybe resolving conflicts. If the locus of control in relational aggression is external, then the locus of control in direct aggression is internal. In terms of gender predispositions, it therefore makes sense why men are inclined to independence, agency and liberty, while women are inclined to dependence, conformity and security. The nature of one's aggression has to align with the nature of one's priorities.

Writing for A Voice for Men, Merrick (2014)[2] introduces us to the relationship between men's self-confidence and exposure to risk, and he contrasts this with the infantilization of women, when we shield them from risk. Accordingly, the infantilization of women predisposes them to diminished confidence and lower self-esteem. I want to expand on Merrick's thesis to add that when one relies on validation from others for their self-esteem, this is an inauthentic, fragile self-esteem that is easily extinguished. Lacking agency and independence, depression is the inevitable state of mind when it all begins to unravel, and one's popularity beings to fade. Depression is the sadness of lacking agency, and feeling overwhelmed by the forces over which you have no control. The psychology of women, with their reliance on networks and the approval of others, with their inclination to the tactics of relational aggression, inherently predisposes women to psychological depression and esteem issues.

Relational aggression is a system of thinking. It's a habit. Each time you practise relational aggression, you are etching the habit ever-deeper. You are re-affirming its truth, and the truth of relational aggression will come back to bite you. What you do to others you do to yourself. If you gossip about others, then when others gossip about you, it comes back to hurt you all the more. Why? Because you yourself have granted gossip its power, when you validated gossip as a legitimate means of hurting others.

The way you judge the world will be the way the world judges you back tenfold. Psychological depression will be your friend when it all starts to go awry. Why? Because you've validated relational damage as the way to move forward. The relational damage you give is the relational damage you get back.

The man that laughs at the world that hates him is a free man, because he's invalidated their reality. He rejects their habits as the habits of fools and the stuff of groupthink. For him, that the world is at Peak Clown is his entertainment, and it poses no threat.

Which brings us to the contemporary manifestation of relational aggression, practised by both men and women, known as cancel culture. Sure, cancel culture can impact adversely on one's career. But the greater concern is less the snowflakes that want to hurt you, than it is the cowardice of those who back down for fear of being called mean names. We shouln't feel any sympathy for the cowards that validate the relational aggression of cowards.

## Relational aggression enters the discourse

The topic of relational aggression first received its impetus in the work of Scandinavians Lagerspetz et al (1988)[3], Bjorqvist (1994)[4], Crick (1995)[5] and Crick & Grotpeter (1995)[6]. Rachel Simmons' book "Odd girl out" (2002)[7] was a pioneering work whose objective was to name the silent crusher of women's souls and give it a face.

The feminist author Phyllis Chesler (2001)[8] provides a comprehensive, academic treatise of the ways in which women strive to destroy women. In her chapter on "Woman's Sexism", for example, she does a fine job of exploring women's interpersonal hostility, revealing their own sexism against women. As she does throughout her book, however, she occasionally reverts to an implicit assumption that women's sexism is reactive to men's sexism.

If we can overlook this predictable bias, given the zeitgeist we live in, her insights are eye-opening. Chesler delves into the deeper psychology of woman-on-woman oppression that explores the envy and hostility in women's relationships with each other, such as that between mother and daughter, sister and sister and, of course, peer to peer.

The destroyers of women's souls are not men. By far the worst annihilators of women's self-esteem are those who understand women best; other women.

# The casualties of relational aggression

The extensive literature on relational aggression brings to light the ways in which women are damaged by relational aggression. Things like low self-esteem, faddism, fearfulness, hatred of women, are all effects suffered by female victims of relational aggression.

### Crushing women's self-esteem through relational aggression

A common thread running through the various literature on relational aggression is the low self-esteem endured by the victims. This low self-esteem can be understood in the context of women's relationship with culture, and their priority to "sustain the cultural known." This relates to questions of philosophy and semiotics that are beyond the scope of this book, and the interested reader is pointed in the direction of Otto Weininger (1906)[9] and Robert Pirsig (1974)[10].

An important aspect of female psychology, more so than it is for men, is to default to the cultural known as a given. For women, the cultural known is "Truth," and failure to measure up to its norms is a personal failure. Hence the low self-esteem suffered by women and girls is soul-destroying. So much so, that when feminists attribute women's low self-esteem to The Patriarchy, it never occurs to the victims to refute it. Women's low self-esteem is the perfect malady to blame on men, simply because women with low self-esteem lack the confidence to refute this myth with the contempt it deserves.

Whether it's anorexia, or bulimia, or depression, these things have little to do with Patriarchal oppression and everything to do with relational aggression visited upon females by females. Even

Naomi Wolf's "Beauty Myth," whilst nurtured and encouraged in aggressive marketing campaigns, owes its success more to the way that women judge each other than anything else. Removing the marketing campaigns or any other aspect of the conspiracy implied in the Patriarchal agenda will *not* eliminate the Beauty Myths by which women aggressively judge each other and exclude those women who fail to measure up to the Beauty Myth's standards.

Relational aggression predisposes women to holding grudges. Thus, where men are predisposed to starting and ending battles quickly, women are inclined to draw them out. Chesler (2001)[11] observes that "girls find physical fights unsatisfactory because they are over too quickly." Throughout her book, she cites several examples of this never-ending, long-suffering battle of wits to which women subject themselves. Sisterly rivalry, mother versus daughter, mother-in-law versus daughter-in-law, harems, all provide her with examples of the silently hostile, combative world that women inhabit.

The focus on relationships that characterizes relational aggression establishes priorities such as popularity, "niceness," conflict-avoidance, politeness and sensitivity. The arsenal of tactics required to maneuver in such a world includes not only gossip, manipulation and exclusion, but also secrecy, diplomacy, silence and deception. Woman's world is one of self-imposed constraints characterized by taboos that establish no-go zones – the shoulds and should-nots by which women police each other's behavior.

The world of relational aggression is a world of restrained emotions, shifting allegiances, sudden outbursts, tears, mistrust, fear, rules and conformity. The niceness and bonhomie by which the shoulds and should-nots of proper behavior are defined and enforced ensure a "peaceful" society where getting along with others is the greatest good. This is a thriving economy where the sharing of secrets and intimacies is the currency with which popularity and social power is aggrandized.

The logics of relational aggression come together in a single condition, a single way of thinking, that we have come to identify as Woman. Left to her own devices, in the absence of Man, the direction of Woman is to the regimented, slavish conformity of the hive. Woman needs Man for her liberation.

The plethora of books and websites that is now available on the topic of relational aggression must inexorably lead to questions about the legitimacy of the feminist mythology behind "patriarchal oppression." Can patriarchal oppression exist in the absence of women's "relational aggression"? More specifically, can patriarchal oppression exist in the absence of the conformity required to make patriarchy work? And if relational aggression is first and foremost a "girl thing," does this not suggest a powerful matriarchal component at work, behind the scenes?

## Esteem and the psychology of relational aggression

The tactics of relational aggression do not usually resonate with the psychology of men. The gender that provides and protects is constantly exposed to risk and danger. Men are constantly putting their lives on the line, in one form or another. Men are constantly testing their assumptions, constantly developing their strategies and their identities. At the cutting edge of cultural evolution, men's survival depends on logic and rationality.

The gender that is protected and provided for, by contrast, is constantly shielded from risk and danger. Women have assumptions passed on to them from their mothers and their peer groups. As creatures of conformity, they rarely have their assumptions tested. Women prefer to assume and conform than to test or compete. Women subscribe to the laws of relational aggression where popularity represents the height of personal achievement. Popularity and not logic or rationality provides the basis for personal esteem.

It is therefore logical that the gender that provides and protects will define itself from a perspective of positive self-esteem, while the best that the protected, provided-for gender can hope to achieve is the less resilient self-esteem grounded in popularity. And when you base your sense of worth on the opinions of others, well, that's hardly empowering, is it. It is impossible to establish a robust sense of self-esteem when narcissism is your passion and popularity provides the foundation on which it is built.

The psychology of women, with their inclination to the tactics of relational aggression, inherently predispose women to psychological depression and esteem issues.

## Like mother, like daughter

Girls, of course, grow up, get married (or, in modern parlance, enter into facto relationships), and leave behind them those horrid, oppressive hierarchies of their adolescence. Or do they?

A woman's marriage to a man might provide her with liberation from all that school-girl nastiness, whether she is perpetrator or victim (or both). But upon pairing up with a man, does a female bully suddenly emerge from her chrysalis to leave behind her past, transforming herself from a self-obsessed, narcissistic, gossiping spoiled brat into a spiritually beautiful butterfly of gentleness and light? Of course not. The habituation of gender roles and gendered personality, enmeshed within the context of culture, tells us that the she-bully remains alive and well; indeed, she thrives. It's just that her priorities have changed. For many she-bullies entering into a more composed adulthood, the priorities of materialism have taken over. And beneath a woman's preoccupation with herself, her house and her creature comforts, her inner adolescent ugliness has reinvented itself and manifests itself in new ways. For example, where in a previous life, she practiced relational aggression, she continues to do so in her new life, only it has become more invisible because her most likely vulnerable victims don't have a voice - they are her children.

Girls in high schools prioritize relationships and connectedness into adulthood. Long after they've transitioned through to adulthood, their social and relationship networks continue to remain at the top of their priorities. They instill these priorities, especially into their daughters.

The scope of the power of Woman is formidable. It is not men who disempower women. It's other women.

## Matriarchal power and culture

### Initial conditions of matriarchal power in culture

If the basis for Matriarchal power and authority is relational aggression, then this has implications for the how the female role as primary nurturer plays out in human cultures.

In the narrative of dynamics systems theory (chaos theory), *initial conditions* relates to the all-important first experiences that establish a template for subsequent development. An infant's earliest life experiences are particularly crucial in establishing the developmental trajectory of the colony of neurons that constitutes its brain, into its functional specializations (Jarosek S. , 2013)[12].

## The hand that rocks the cradle rules the world

In most cultures, Mother is the primary nurturer. Mother provides the greatest influence upon the initial conditions to which a child is subjected - the initial conditions that have the greatest influence on how a young, malleable brain develops in the formative years. The first choices that an infant makes are controlled primarily by Mother. Clearly, the role of Woman as mother is far from trivial. Matriarchal power reaches its tentacles into children's formative years, irrespective of whether the cultural-religious background of said matriarchy is Islamic, Christian, Buddhist or Hindu.

The hand that rocks the cradle? Maybe it's a stretch to say that it rules the world. Then again, maybe it's not. One thing we can say for certain - men do not have free reign. Men do not operate in a vacuum. They do have another formidable power to answer to.

# Bully-victim duality

Are we not yet convinced of the vindictive, destructive nature of relational aggression? Do we think that it is somehow a "nicer," more benign form of nastiness than "direct" aggression? Then it would pay us to take a closer look at the relationship that exists between victims and the bullies that they choose, or the crime-prone children that they raise.

Before we immerse ourselves further into this topic, we should note that the bully-victim duality is a complex one with many nuances. The popular feminist trope of men bullying women, for example within the context of domestic violence, represents only a small sampling of the many contexts that play out in reality. There is also female-on-male domestic violence. And of course, there is child abuse.

But it is also true to say that in the context of gender roles, women have a preference for dominant, successful men. One could argue that the bully-victim duality is etched into our chromosomes and extends to culture's gender roles, with the suggestion that nature predisposes men to take advantage of women. The implication being that the state must intervene to protect the so-called "vulnerable." We should take a closer look at this duality, to understand why it is much more complex than the widely-accepted, feminist victim-trope would have us believe.

It should also be pointed out that there is a deeper, almost metaphysical, dimension to complicity in one's own bullying. In complicity, the victim validates the bully, validates the narrative and its duality. Victim really does become bully not as a figurative rationalization, but in real sense where they act out the bully within on those weaker than themselves. This is an important point that is not widely understood. The bully-victim duality is complex, and I certainly cannot give it all the attention that it deserves, in these few pages.

Let us briefly recap on the nature and extent of matriarchal authority, and the importance of the primary nurturer in defining the things that matter:

- What is it that is behind the gynocentrism that characterizes western culture (and arguably, all cultures)? What is "first cause," the primary reason? It is the primary nurturer. It is under the primary nurturer's care that most of a child's neuroplastic brain is wired; as we've discussed in previous chapters, 90% of a human brain's wiring is accomplished within the first four years of life. And in most cultures throughout most of human history, the primary nurturer has tended to be the mother;

- Exactly the same principles apply in reverse. Raise an animal among humans, and you get a domesticated pet. Raise a human infant, from birth, among wild animals, like wolves, and you get a feral child (Wikipedia, 2016)[13];

- If it is mostly mothers that wire brains, then the role of fathers, by contrast, is best understood in the context of cultural evolution and improvement, and undoing the baggage of imperfect wiring. Remember, before feminism, when it was permissible to talk about schizophrenogenic mothers? Cultural traditions and religions have always placed man in the more spiritual role. This is the role of freeing oneself of the mother's and the culture's definitions;

- Given the role of the primary nurturer, it would seem self-evident that children first learn violence from their primary nurturer. It is well established that women play as crucial a role in child abuse as men do, and children learn what their parents teach them. Imitation is one of the most important vehicles for learning;

- Matriarchal subcultures are closely interconnected with the violence in their cultures not only in the children that they raise, but also the thugs that they choose. Thugs resonate as much with the abusive natures of the women that choose them as with the women that raise them. Like with like, and all that. What goes around comes around;

- The very success of feminism is itself an expression of the power of a bullying matriarchal authority that has escaped proper scrutiny in our cultures of politically correct, anti-male wokeness and neo-Darwinian determinism;

- Even in cultures said to have the worst reputations in the world for denying women their rights, matriarchs wield considerable influence in defining the conduct that is to be expected of their children. Muslim women, for example, are not the wilting wallflowers of feminist propaganda. The life of a suicide bomber may be short and brutal, but he will occupy a special place of pride in his mother's memory, and she will honor the son who gave his life in the name of Allah;

## Bully-victim narrative

We just saw, under the topic of relational aggression, how the infantilization of women predisposes them to self-esteem issues (Merrick, 2014)[14], which in turn impacts on the dynamic between the submissive and the dominant. This, in turn, impacts on the choices that women make, and explains a great deal about women's preferences.

Much has been written about the power of the tyrant, and how a tyrant can only earn respect by being tyrannical. The willing deference of submissives to those that dominate them is a well-established psychological phenomenon, as it relates to the bully-victim narrative. The complicity of submissives within the context of oppression comes under different labels, depending on one's agenda. For example, there is the Stockholm Syndrome (Layton, 2006)[15]. Other writers make reference to the bully-victim narrative in the context of cultures, for example, violent-passive tribes, why thuggish rulers are respected more than peaceful ones, etc. It is generally accepted that there is no such thing as a gentle, respectful tyrant. One example from Elias Canetti's (1973) *Crowds and Power*[16]:

> One of the main attributes of an African king was his absolute power over life and death. The terror that he spread was tremendous. 'You are now Ata, you have power over life and death. Kill everyone who says he does not fear you': thus the formula of investiture of the king of Igara. He killed as he pleased and gave no reason. His wish was sufficient; he did not have to account for it. In many cases he was not allowed to shed blood himself, but the executioner who did it for him was the one indispensable official of his court. Whether the man who started by occupying that office ultimately became Prime Minister, as in Dahomey, or whether there were hundreds of executioners who formed a kind of caste, as in Ashanti; whether executions were frequent or were limited to occasional cases, the pronouncement of death sentences was always the undisputed right of the king and if he let any considerable time pass without exercising it the terror essential to his power was lost; he was no longer feared, but was held in contempt.
>
> (Canetti, p. 423)

The last sentence is key "... he was no longer feared, but was held in contempt." This bully-victim dynamic plays out not only in violent tribes in far-off places, but also in modern democracies and in households characterized by violence, whether between a woman and a man, or a parent and their child. A woman's preference for thugs does not magically materialize from a vacuum. She knows what she wants and she knows how to get it. Let us unpack this to properly understand it.

Perhaps without realizing it, PUA Game is an attempt to harness the submissive-dominant narrative with the intention to manipulate women. Summarizing the main implications of the submissive-dominant narrative, as it applies to female psychology and the kinds of choices to which they are predisposed to making:

- Even though it is the formidable in man to which women are most drawn, it is also the formidable in man that spooks them. Which makes sense when you think about it, because it relates to the very nature of the sexual tension that exists between male and female. A brute presents the perfect solution when a woman feels ill at ease. While there is little to be expected of a brute, there is little to get worked up about. There is no anticipation of loss to fear because there is little to lose. Everyone's much more relaxed and at peace with the world, and this primes her for submission and earns him an easy notch;

- When a woman chooses a brute, she validates him. She is casting her vote in favor of what she thinks all men should be. And her children acquire the training necessary to carry on the family tradition into future generations. Spreading the karma, as it were;

- From a woman's choices, other women learn what's hot, and men learn what works. Many PUAs get their cues for behavior from the idiots that women choose. Instead of laughing at women's dopey choices, PUAs want to *become* women's dopey choices. It gets them laid, I guess, but at what cost?

- One often reads of women choosing bad boys with the intention of trying to convert them. From the preceding discussion, we can see how this would work. Women spook when they encounter the formidable in man. Many would rather try to convert an emotionally stunted adolescent who is non-threatening than relate to a self-assured adult who knows himself;

- Another reason that I've seen a woman admit to, to explain her stupid choice, is that she won't be disappointed to let him go. Hello? What manner of hellscape is this? Has she not heard of hobbies, like cooking, or origami?

- With the absence of risk in the lives of kept women, with being provided for, affirmative action, employment as a hobby, work as something to do if you like, something you do if your fancy takes you, things must get boring pretty quickly. In a life untested, without challenges, it is inevitable that the deferential (submissive) role will more likely fall to women than to men;

- Further to the absence of risk in women's indulgent, provided-for lives, choosing a thug can provide spice to an otherwise predictable routine, it annoys over-controlling parents and sends a clear message for them to back off, and it draws attention to oneself as an innocent victim;

- Within the context of the bully-victim narrative, submissives will also be bullies to those that cannot defend themselves - i.e., their children; hence the statistics bearing out the fact that women are the primary abusers of children;

- From Canetti's passage, "... he [the tyrant] was no longer feared, but was held in contempt." A consistent narrative for a woman who inexplicably finds herself sipping latte with a deferential beta instead of sculling beer with an exciting brute would be along the lines, "There must be something wrong with him for believing that I am worthy... what a loser." Many a brute is instinctively aware that a good thrashing can bring his errant spouse back into line, and he realizes that she won't respect anything less. Of course the odds are that he probably learned this first from his primary nurturer and the context in which he grew up;

- Women often conflate manliness with "degenerate" or "animal." The more brutish a man, the hotter, to many a woman, he must be. What can be manlier than a mumbling gorilla lunging a grope? The idea of the formidable man as poet, or inventor, or leader,  or discoverer is alien to many women's mindsets;

- Often a brute is profitable; Hypergamy 1:001. A brute with money is less likely to question his existence or her motives, and Material-Girl will often overlook his obvious flaws and regard him as an appropriate lifestyle choice. This puts Material-Girl in the driver's seat, where she is in control of whether she stays or leaves. Grrrl power and all that;

- Last but certainly not least is the thrill of the forbidden - more specifically, the cultural forbidden. The forbidden lies at the interface between the cultural known and the unknown. A brute with attitude, as the kind of man that her parents used to warn her about, can stir a woman's primal motivations in ways that a deferential beta cannot.

Of course not all women choose brutes. Far from it. But it is important to understand that when a woman does choose a thug, she's making an active choice. She may not be consciously aware of what she is looking for; she may be unable to articulate it, but her primal motivations guide her choices as surely as a missile's guidance system zeroes in on its target. Often she may not know, in the early days, that he's actually a thug, but she will be drawn to the dominant and/or the profitable in him. To this kind of woman, a deferential beta won't get a look-in. Contrary to what popular lore would have us believe, Woman is not a helpless wallflower being preyed on by opportunistic, clever men. It is a strange irony indeed that feminists don't see the misogyny behind their presumption of women as lame and without agency. Back in the sixties during the emergence of contemporary feminism, feminists used to spit on the chivalrous, suited chumps that would open car doors for them. These days, it would make more sense, in their self-loathing misogyny, for them to spit on themselves.

# 3.2 WOMEN AS OPPRESSORS

## The oppression of women by women

For nearly half a century, feminism has peddled the myth of the oppression of women by men. This myth would normally have been regarded as so completely baseless that the only reasonable response would have been to ignore it or laugh at it. To respond to it is to give it a credibility that it does not deserve.

But the myth has sculpted reality, and the personal is political. This myth has created laws, regulations and assumptions that now direct our lives – laws, regulations and assumptions whose foundations are as solid as… thin air. For this reason, we need to state the obvious. Here, I provide a cursory overview of the oppression that never was.

## Female Genital Mutilation

Amnesty International (Female genital mutilation)[17] recognizes that Female Genital Mutilation (FGM) is, in the majority of cases, women doing it to women. On their website, they suggest that "usually only women are allowed to be present." Perhaps this understates a rather harsher truth. A little further research finds that it is, for all intents and purposes, *always* women doing it to women, in the course of sacred women's rituals and sacred rites of passage. And so irrespective of whatever ghostly influence men and "The Patriarchy" are purported to have, it would appear that in most cases, it is adult women taking young girls to the sacred sites. It is adult women holding them down, to prevent them from moving, and adult women holding their legs apart to allow the knife to cut. And it is *always* a woman wielding the cutting implement.

The Female Genital Cutting Education and Networking Project (2003)[18] references Chapter 6 of Jomo Kenyatta's book (1965)[19]. They provide about as impartial, objective an account of the process as can be hoped for, given the times we live in. And consistent with the norm, it is clear that FGM is part of a sacred women's ritual, with female surgeons performing the clitoridectomy, with female sponsors and female villagers participating in the celebrations. As per Kenyatta's example, FGM is a girl's rite of passage (just as boys have their own rite of passage, when fathers remove them from the tribe, to be introduced to the ways of men):

> The initiation of both sexes is the most important custom among the Gikuyu. It is looked upon as a deciding factor in giving a boy or girl the status of manhood or womanhood in the Gikuyu community. This custom is adhered to by the vast majority of African peoples and is found in almost every part of the continent.

FGM has nothing to do with patriarchal oppression of women. FGM is a Kenyan form of "sacred women's business" (*sacred women's business* is an established term that refers to Australian aboriginal traditions where young girls go with their women elders to be introduced to the ways of adult women). FGM is how women of some cultures, rightly or wrongly, celebrate their girls becoming women. If feminists insist on stating this in the victim-oppressor terms that they are familiar with, then let there be no ambiguity; FGM is women brutalizing women.

## Persecution of witches - Salem witch trials

In the history of the persecution of witches, we have further examples of women oppressing women. Inasmuch as men, as decision-makers (judges, law enforcement, etc), most often provided the visible face of the persecution of "witches," the truth is rather more complex. Let us, for example, briefly look at the Salem witch trials of the late 17th century in America.

Witches were primarily identified and tried on the basis of testimonies provided by witnesses who were "afflicted" (afflicted by dreams, premonitions). Without going into the interesting details concerning the role of gossip (a primarily female activity), let us briefly take a look at some of the statistics. The Salem Witch Trials website (Siteclopedia: Salem Witch Trials, 2000)[20] provides some numbers. All up, 37 of the afflicted were female, and 5 were male. 5 of the afflicted were from 1 to 10 years old, and 27 of them were from 11 to 20 years old. 34 were single, 7 were married. By a process of elimination, we might begin to see a typical profile emerge (i.e., how does single female between 11 and 20 years old, sound?). As many of the afflicted were children, we might expect the primary nurturer to have had some measure of input.

Now, let's look at the Salem trials from a slightly different perspective. 14 women and 5 men were executed. A sixth man was "pressed" (crushed by stone weights) for refusing to admit innocence or guilt. 200 people were awaiting trial before the process was declared unlawful, and they were subsequently released. What was the role of gossip, a primarily female activity, in identifying the other 200? The majority of the witnesses, as the afflicted, were girls and young women. In this light, 14 women and 6 men murdered cannot constitute a statistically significant proof that the Salem community practiced single-minded oppression against women perpetrated solely by men.

As a side-note, do we notice the parallels between the afflicted witnesses of the Salem witch trials whose testimonies are based solely on dreams and premonitions, and the contemporary practice of accepting at face value the unsubstantiated allegations of a woman accusing a man of rape, while preserving her anonymity? The modern rape accuser would appear to be the contemporary manifestation of the Salem witch trials' afflicted witness.

## The hijab and burka

The hijab (veil) is a cultural tradition actively insisted upon by women. Muslim women know that they *want* to wear the veil and any denial of this simple fact trivializes them and their choices.

There is no ambiguity, no misogynist conspiracy to consider in Muslim women's desire to wear the veil. Since French President Jacques Chirac announced his ban on headscarves, thousands of women wearing the hijab have marched in protest across France, chanting slogans such as "Not our fathers, nor our husbands, we chose the headscarf" (Smith, 2004)[21]. Muslim women actively support most every legitimate aspect of their Islamic faith, including the hijab. You can count on it, that as many Muslim women (the nurturers of sons and the wives of men) support suicide bombing as do Muslim men.

Writing for Time, Richard Lacayo (2001)[22] is perplexed by the apparent acceptance by many Afghan women of the burka (head-to-toe covering worn in Afghanistan), and then tries to explain it away in terms of the presence of men:

> Many rural women, especially, claim to wear it willingly, at least when they speak in the presence of their husbands. There is even high fashion in burka wear. In Kabul, women allow a bit of lace trimming to show at the edge. The best burkas, from the Afghan city of Herat, have exquisite pleating that imparts a shimmering, watery feel but takes hours to iron. But nearly any educated woman loathes the burka. So do many less educated ones - if you can question them where men cannot hear.

Mr Lacayo's disappointment in the apparent complicity of Muslim women is evident in his unsubstantiated claims and definitions. Consistent with feminist dogma, he perceives anti-woman conspiracies where there are none - for example, in his comment "… at least when they speak in the presence of their husbands." And on what terms does he define "educated woman"? Might he mean educated in Women's Studies, or at a Western (read "pro-feminist") university?

## Other examples of women oppressing women

Gendercide Watch (2012)[23] provides many examples of gendercide that go well beyond the Western orthodoxy based in the assumption that women are oppressed by men.

- The European witch-hunts: These were collaborative efforts between men and women. Gendercide Watch (2012)[24], with references to Deborah Willis' book, *Malevolent Nurture* and to Robin Gibbs' book, *Witches & Neighbours* discusses the European witch-hunts noting that:

> In fact, the stigmatizing, victimizing, and murdering of accused 'witches' is more accurately seen as a collaborative enterprise between men and women at the local level. 'The historical record suggests that both men and women found it easiest to fix these fantasies (of witchcraft), and turn them into horrible reality, when they were attached to women. It is really crucial to understand that misogyny in this sense was not reserved to men alone, but could be just as intense among women.' Most of the accusations originated in 'conflicts (that) normally opposed one woman to another, with men liable to become involved only at a later stage as ancillaries to the original dispute.' Briggs adds that 'most informal accusations were made by women against other women, … (and only) leaked slowly across to the men who controlled the political structures of local society.'

In other words, men did the dirty-work of women, who oppressed other women through relational aggression.

- Sati (bride-burning in India): There have been examples in the Indian media where women have revolted against attempts to deny them this sacred women's rite. Sati and bride murder are also blamed, in large part, on economic "necessity" (the dowry system of India) and the problems associated with providing for women without husbands. And as such, newspaper reports implicating women (e.g., mothers-in-law) as often as men should come as no surprise.

- Killing of female children (infanticide): With feminism controlling the cultural agenda, the role of mothers is rarely mentioned. Yet, if we acknowledge the fact that the killing of female children is based in economic "necessity," as girls will never grow up to become good providers, we might expect mothers to be at least equally implicated. And so it follows that women would be the primary perpetrators of infanticide - *Milner* (1998)[25] and *Kunkle* (2014)[26]. Gendercide Watch (2012)[27] observes that "Infanticide is a crime overwhelmingly committed by women, both in the Third and First Worlds." Furthermore, Gendercide Watch (2012) quotes Brian Woods from The Dying Rooms Trust (1995)[28]:

> [...] culture dictates that when a girl marries she leaves her family and becomes part of her husband's family. For this reason Chinese peasants have for many centuries wanted a son to ensure there is someone to look after them in their old age -- having a boy child is the best pension a Chinese peasant can get. Baby girls are even called 'maggots in the rice'.

In third-world countries that are less inclined to indulge in the Happy Families Delusion that afflicts the Anglosphere, children are more likely to be regarded as a necessary investment. Mothers in third-world countries know that their sons are more productive in the paddy-fields for longer periods of time than their daughters – sons make better, more reliable providers. Sons are the substitute welfare in cultures that do not provide welfare pensions in old age. Their priority for boys is nothing other than cold, pragmatic survival. Boy as rice-paddy laborer grows to be man as provider. Arguably, infanticide is more a matriarchal than a patriarchal phenomenon, because it is the *mother* who decides who shall live and who shall die. It is the *mother* who giveth life and it is the *mother* who taketh away.

# The oppression of men by women

## In the service of Woman

There are the ways in which women oppress men, manipulating them and shaming them into doing what women would otherwise do if men refused to subscribe to their chivalrist obligations. Some examples follow.

Provided-for women who were never conscripted to fight wars, nonetheless thought nothing of pinning white feathers on the "cowardly" men who refused to fight (Beckett (2008)[29] and Gullace (2014)[30]). Do we see anything wrong with this picture?

What was the source of the power of women that compelled men to give up their seats on the lifeboats of the Titanic? How has this come to pass, that the gender that was never required to design or build boats, ships, buildings, aircraft or houses, the gender that was never required to labor in mines or fight wars or provide for families, should be the gender with first priority to the life-boats, the gender to pin white feathers on the "cowards" who refused to fight their wars?

## Violence by proxy

What is the source of the power of women that has men doing their dirty-work? For the truth is that men also do the dirty-work of women, who are too comfortable in the security provided by men to be bothered to do it themselves.

Briefly, but importantly, women's psychology is predisposed to preserving cultural traditions; that is, the cultural known. In this role, theirs is the power of veto; the authority that blocks deviations from the cultural known. These dynamics relate to phenomenology and existentialism and further detailed discussion is beyond the scope of this book. However, from these important principles, we can thus infer that women are the sustainers of the cultural known, and they are the filters of cultural variety.

Thus, in this capacity (sustaining the cultural known, filtering the cultural unknown), women choose the types of men that they would like their sons to be - *the types of men most likely to do their bidding*. When a woman, in her priority to be provided for, acquiesces to make her pact with the devil, she is an accomplice and a partner in crime. She has cast her vote in favor of what she thinks all men should be.

Women get men, and the system, to do violence against men on their behalf. For example, when a woman makes a false allegation of rape, she is using other men and/or the system to harm another man.

Would a woman lie about rape? The simple facts, buttressed by statistics, do indeed confirm that women lie about rape, and they do so to a frightening degree. Marc Angelucci and Glenn Sacks (2004)[31] review several reliable studies and reports to confirm that false allegations of rape occur anywhere between 25% and 50% of the time. For example:

> According to a nine-year study conducted by former Purdue sociologist Eugene J. Kanin, in over 40 percent of the cases reviewed, the complainants eventually admitted that no rape had occurred.

Referring to a study of 556 rape allegations conducted by the USA Air Force, an investigation by independent reviewers found that 60 percent of the original rape allegations were false. Canvassing several reliable sources, Angelucci and Sacks establish that the true percentage of false allegations for rape far exceeds the 2% figure commonly promoted by the media. This less realistic figure, they point out, can be attributed to feminist Susan Brownmiller, who was relaying the alleged comments of a New York judge regarding the rate of false rape allegations in a New York City police precinct in 1974, rather than referencing any kind of reliable study or analysis.

In any war or conflict, women are conducting violence by proxy when they urge their sons or husbands to fight. They are also conducting violence by proxy when, as participants in the economy, they are purchasers and consumers of the materials or goods over which their country's wars are ultimately fought. Yet women get off scot-free.

During the atrocities perpetrated in Afghanistan in around 2001, for example, large numbers of Hazara men and boys were slaughtered by the Taliban in preemptive raids, in order to cull the numbers of a potential enemy. And the media barely rated it a mention. We heard little in the media of the large numbers of men and boys who fled Afghanistan in order to avoid forced conscription by the Taliban. Why did we hear so much more about widows and so little about the men and boys who lost their lives? Was the sight of a crying woman supposed to be more heart-wrenching than a battle-ground littered with rotting male corpses?

## Do as your mother tells you

On Australian Sixty Minutes on Richard Carlton's report on suicide bombers (Carlton, 2001)[32], a Palestinian woman declared, raising her voice, trying to convince the ignorant westerner, who just didn't seem to "get it," that she *wants* her son to die, to become a hero for the Arab cause - as the camera panned across to the innocent face of a little boy not even into his teens.

In *The Australian* newspaper, Natalie O'Brien's[33] front-page headline (2005) reads "Mum's permission needed for terror plan." Quoting from evidence before Sydney's Central Local Court, spiritual leader Abdul Nacer Benbrika is quoted as saying, "Some people claim to love jihad but don't respect their own parents... You need permission from your parents to go to jihad. If your mother says no to jihad, then no jihad." Two days later, Mazen Touma (alleged to have been training for jihad) asked for his mother's permission to undertake jihad. Her response did not appear in the police evidence, and she refused to speak to the media.

This, is the power of mother over son. The sustainer of the known provides the framework to which a boy will refer in his transition into manhood. The sustainer of the known will provide the goals and standards that boys and men will feel obligated to uphold and carry out. Motherhood, femininity, provides the basis for the cultural known around which the explorers of the unknown will gravitate and test the limits. The power of the hand that rocks the cradle is formidable. It is from the mother that an infant growing into childhood first learns about the things that matter.

# The oppression of children by women

We've already seen how women are the primary perpetrators of infanticide. Let us shed some more light on the role of men and women in the abuse of children.

From Child Maltreatment (2002)[34] (CM 2002), a document published by the Department of Health and Human Services in the United States, women comprised 58.3% of the perpetrators of child abuse and men comprised 41.7% (Figure 5-1 of CM 2002 and accompanying Table 5-1, Age and Sex of Perpetrators[35]). Most of the abuse of children (Table 5-3 of CM 2002[36]) was broken down as follows:

- 53.3% of all perpetrators neglected children;
- 11.0% of all perpetrators physically abused children;
- 6.9% of all perpetrators sexually abused children.

Women were more likely to neglect children, while men were more likely to abuse children.

32.6% of child fatalities were perpetrated by the mother acting alone, while 16.6% of child fatalities were perpetrated by the father acting alone (Figure 4-2 of CM 2002, Fatalities by Perpetrator Relationship[37]). That is to say:

*Approximately twice as many mothers as fathers are responsible for the fatalities of their children.*

Why does the fact that women are the primary abusers of children seem to surprise many of us? After all, it is already well established that:

*Infanticide and Munchausen's syndrome by proxy are crimes overwhelmingly perpetrated by women.*

## Closing comment on reporting inconsistencies

The above analysis was undertaken some time ago and so in the interests of objectivity, we briefly examine the most recent Child Maltreatment report available at this time of writing (CM 2011, published 2012). These more recent figures show some variation from the 2002 report. According to CM 2011 (2012)[38]:

- 53.6% of perpetrators of child abuse were women, while 45.1 percent of perpetrators were men (as opposed to the 58.3% versus 41.7% in CM 2002);
- Nearly two-fifths (36.8%) of maltreatment victims were maltreated by their mother acting alone (compared against 40.3% in CM 2002);
- One-fifth (19.0%) of maltreatment victims were maltreated by their father acting alone (compared against 19.1% in CM 2002);
- 26.4% of child fatalities were perpetrated by the mother acting alone (compared against 32.6% in CM 2002);
- 15.3% of child fatalities were perpetrated by the father acting alone (compared against 16.6% in CM 2002);

While the CM 2011 report appears to suggest some amelioration of gender differences in perpetrator compared to the CM 2002 report, other evidence gleaned from around the internet (e.g., the Mary Kellett corruption scandal in Maine (Elam, 2011)[39]) seems to increasingly suggest systemic breakdown, and it is not clear to what extent we can continue to trust an affirmative-action, woman-friendly, misandric industry that implements research that might be contrary to its own agenda. We should anticipate that records will become increasingly less reliable as our cultural systems continue their death spiral.

## The neglect of child abuse

How has this come to pass that women are the primary abusers of children, yet the domestic violence (dv) industry continues to persist with the myth of men as the primary abusers of both women *and children*? Here's the reason:

- Children do not get in our faces. They don't know how to raise our conscious awareness regarding their plight. They don't go on marches to take back the night.
- Children do not form lobby groups to influence politicians. They do not write to newspapers to voice outrage in the

media at the injustices perpetrated against them by their primary abuser.

- Children don't know how to assert their rights. They don't know how to seek protection in dv shelters.

Abused children must bear their pain in silence, because when they no longer have their parents to protect them, they have no way of being heard.

## The importance of the primary nurturer

Ultimately, what we can conclude is that the role of Woman is not that of trivial, helpless bystander. Child abuse, whether by neglect or by physical/sexual abuse, results in child fatalities and in this, we see that the mother's role is far from trivial.

As we've touched on throughout this book, women have always had real power that is in no way to be considered anything less than male power. Some might argue that Woman's power is greater, for ultimately, the sustainer of the known has privileged access to those who are most vulnerable - her children. So perhaps there might be some justification for the historical view that:

*The hand that rocks the cradle rules the world.*

The myth of patriarchal oppression is a myth that trivializes the power of Woman. It is not the patriarchy that makes women invisible, but feminism.

## Mother continues to wield her influence on adult men

As discussed in some detail in previous chapters, mothers as primary nurturers play a crucial role in defining the things that matter, and subsequently, how brains are wired. Let us revisit this topic briefly in order to get a clearer picture of why Mother's influence persists into adulthood, and why even adult men continue to defer to Womankind, despite her slighter, less threatening physique. This is important if we are to properly apprehend the source of feminine power and thus, the persistence of matriarchal tyranny.

The importance of the primary nurturer extends beyond the context of child abuse and into the realms of phenomenology and existentialism. It is from our primary nurturer that we first learn about the things that matter.

Mother as primary nurturer provides the basis for the initial conditions around which the infant brain-as-sponge self-organizes. Just as a large animal, like a lion, tiger, killer whale or elephant, raised from birth, readily succumbs to the commands of a much smaller trainer, so too the larger man succumbs to the commands of a smaller primary nurturer - that loomed so large when he was a helpless infant.

Mothers have always been the primary trainers taming their dependent children. In men, this manifests in culture by subduing males into servile obedience[*]. Chivalry and the tendency for men to recoil in horror at the thought of raising a hand to Woman can be understood from the perspective of matriarchal, motherly power that trains male infants in the fundamentals of proper social conduct. Chivalry is the manifestation in adult men of what was first encountered as love and fear of Mother.

Let's put it another way. Sigmund Freud identified what he called the Oedipus Complex. In psychoanalytic theory, a man "suffering" from an Oedipus Complex retains an unhealthy (sexual) attraction for his mother. It is incorrect, however, to designate this as an "affliction" of *some* men, because it overlooks the real importance that Woman-as-Mother has on the lives of *all* men. The Oedipus "Complex" is not a complex at all, but a fundamental expression of the ground from which Man emerges, and the ground to which he looks for support in adulthood. It becomes a "complex" only when a man fails to liberate himself from obsessive, indulgent motherly influences. This is the reason why adult male role models are so important for adolescent boys. It is the reason for the direct, causative relationship between single-mother households and crime (Baskerville, 1999)[40].

---

[*] Fathers also play a central role in disciplining children, especially as they grow into adolescence.

# The oppression of daughters by women

Chesler's analysis of the mother-daughter relationship is insightful and often chilling. How is it that we find ourselves in this surreal situation purporting men to be the primary abusers of women and children, when in fact the reality is so different?

Chesler (2001)[41] writes that "In many nineteenth-century families, mothers, even more than fathers, disciplined their children, daughters especially." She then quotes documented examples of whippings and beatings administered by mothers. On the psychological impact of mother-inflicted beatings, Chesler (2001) [42] observes:

> Although it is true that fathers (and society) expected mothers to 'whip their daughters into obedience' and therefore shared responsibility for the whippings, nevertheless, because those whippings were actually administered by mothers, the psychological effect was female-specific and had long-range psychological consequences.

Indeed, a lot of mother-inflicted abuse seems to have a strong psychological component. Chesler refers to the "Stockholm Syndrome" when discussing how "an abused child or adult hostage may cling to her abusive parent or captor."

Chesler quotes Bertha Harris, a Professor of Literature: "I was myself so ashamed of being my mother's victim, and of my helplessness in her power, I made every attempt to conceal the facts of my early life from intimates, even from myself." What might be the carry-over effects of a woman's relationship with her mother, to feminism? A suggestion is proffered, before it is muted: "I will go to any amount of trouble to help a woman get what she says she wants; if I must sacrifice something I want in the process, so much the better. Sometimes this behavior is mistaken for feminism; it is penance."

Chesler's (2001) [43] memory of her mother probably reflects that of many people: "My mother was my Chief Criticizer, Threatener, Belittler, Screamer, Pincher, Hair-Puller, and Twisted-Red-Faced-Terrifier. 'I'm telling your father what you did. He'll take care of you'. She did not administer the serious beatings; she forced my father to do that." Chesler reminisces on her mother's pride and nostalgia for her father: "Oy, did he have a bad temper! He always had to arrive first to a wedding. We had to jump when he snapped his finger! Would he yell!"

Elsewhere, Chesler acknowledges the power of Mother to force Father's hand. In exploring how daughters in incestuous families are betrayed by their mothers, she provides some sense of the complex (systemic) dynamics that take place in domestic violence. For example, she relates the story of sixteen-year-old Rose Wilson who, in 1988, shot her mother Martha in the head following eleven years of abuse by three men (one of whom was Martha's husband, Roger Wilson). Rose's mother had not only refused to protect her from the rapes and beatings, but she actually encouraged her husband to beat Rose.

Psychological abuse of daughters is implied when Chesler (2001) [44] writes:

> Many twentieth-century mothers have violated their adolescent daughters' boundaries with impunity. They have secretly read their daughters' locked diaries, steamed open their mail, listened in on their phone calls. Thus, daughters become used to being patrolled by an intimate avenger.

On maternal envy (of daughters), Chesler (2001) [45] writes:

> In my view, maternal envy teaches many daughters how *not* to be a threat to other women. In addition, maternal envy teaches daughters to be passive, fearful, conformist, obedient - as well as similarly cruel to other women.

Anorexia, bulimia, all the purported manifestations of women's low self-esteem... can they really come from an oppressive patriarchy... from men who know so little of female psychology? Wouldn't a bullying matriarchy be closer to the mark? Is it not more accurate to say that men are the *saviors* of women rather than their tormentors? Is not marriage to a man to be regarded as escape into fresh air in comparison to this relentless matriarchal oppression to which daughters are often exposed from infancy?

# The validation of violence by women

There exists another category of oppression that all too often flies under the radar. It is the vicarious oppression that emerges through complicity. When women choose thugs, rapists and murderers, they are validating criminal conduct. Their choices are votes in favor of the types of men that they think all men should be. These choices become votes for what the culture stands for.

Men and women inhabit different universes, and the primal nature of human sexuality that accounts for it, can be expressed in a simple example. An ugly, mumbling degenerate with a boner can do for women what no ugly, overweight whore in ovulation can ever do for men. Women's rape fantasies encompass contexts that are alien to men. There is something about female sexuality that predisposes to self-harm in a way that male sexuality does not. Beauty and submission are integral to female sexuality, and achievement and dominance are integral to men's. This plays out in the sexual dynamics between men and women and the choices that they make, and invariably brings us to the question of why many women are often drawn to violent men.

## Criminals and the women who love them

In the Special Report section of The Guardian newspaper, Denise Mina (2003)[46] asks "Why are women drawn to men behind bars?".

It seems inconceivable to normal people why any sane, well-adjusted woman would want to marry a murderer. Yet the reality is that this happens all too frequently, as The Guardian article explores. This happens to the extent where criminals sometimes attain some kind of celebrity status - for example, Ian Huntley, the man from Soham, who was charged with the murders of schoolgirls Jessica Chapman and Holy Wells, receives bundles of fan mail from women every week.

And as Mina points out, "the cliché of the prison bride as wig-wearing trailer-trash is misguided: the women come from all sectors of society." She provides further examples of notorious, celebrity-status criminals such as Richard Ramirez (the Night Stalker who murdered and dismembered 13 people in the 1980s was married in 1996 in prison), and Ted Bundy (suspected of murdering 35 young women) - noting that they attracted gangs of admiring groupies who sat patiently through their court cases. Carlos the Jackal became engaged to his lawyer in 2002. And John Wayne Gacy, with a history of drugging, raping and murdering 30 men in Chicago, married while he was awaiting the death penalty.

It is tempting to write off these relationships as aberrations - deviations from the norm. This would be a mistake, for it would deny us a valuable insight into female sexuality. I think it would be more instructive to regard these relationships as *primal manifestations* of the norm, rather than deviations from it.

Mina lists some theories to explain the appeal that criminals have for women:

- Isenberg (2000)[47] suggests vicarious murder as sometimes a possible motivating factor - that is, living out the intent to murder in their choice of men. Quoting Isenberg, Mina writes:

  > Even while she denies his culpability, it is his ability to murder that attracts her. He acted on his rage, however unsuitably. [The woman] could never act on her rage. So [his] murder is [her] murder.

- There is the account of Avril and Rose, who left long-term "boring" marriages for men in prison (Avril was killed by her lover, while Rose's husband was back in prison after trying to cut her ear off, and pulling her teeth out with pliers);
- Hybristophilia - this is a paraphilia (sexual perversion) characterized by sexual arousal and orgasm that are contingent upon being with a partner known to have committed a crime of violence, such as murder, rape or armed robbery;
- The fantasy element of the romance is allowed to proceed without ever translating to the messiness and "ordinariness of sex and marriage."

## Rape fantasies and the thrill of the forbidden

But there exists another dimension of female sexuality that can shed further light on the appeal that criminals have for women and the subsequent votes that women cast in the choices that they make. It ties in with women's inclination to fantasize about rape (Castleman (2010)[48], Hutson (2008)[49]). What we are considering here is the primal nature of female sexuality.

In her Diary II, Anaïs Nin (1970)[50] wrote, "to be violated is perhaps a need in a woman, a secret erotic need." The theme of violation is a persistent one that crops up throughout Nin's writings. Her stories focus on man as possessor and woman as possessed, of man as violator and woman as violated. It therefore follows that the context of a woman's longing to be violated requires a violator. A violator resonates with something in women's primal sexual motivations.

The thrill of the forbidden, in female sexuality, is the thrill of throwing it away. And throwing it away carries within it the seed of self-destruction. When she's choosing a confident, handsome, wealthy leader with connections, she's not throwing anything away. When she's choosing from among her social circles, or club meetings, or church gatherings, or workplace, she's not throwing anything away. But when she submits in delirious abandon to a raucous rabble or a degenerate stranger that makes her perhaps more than a little afraid, that is when she is throwing something away.

Like a roller-coaster ride, the fear of the unknown is a spice that women find exhilarating. How they act on that fear is all-important, because it defines their character, their circles and their future. The thrill of the forbidden, as the thrill of throwing it away, is as self-destructive as it is destructive to culture and society.

And in understanding the primal nature of female sexuality, we are better equipped to understand why feminist women notice and obsess about the worst among men. They are projecting; they are acting out what gets them all hot, bothered and excited about the brutes among men. All while the majority of men who are decent, responsible and kind are invisible to them. There is something about the worst among men that many women find arousing; perhaps it is the violator in women's rape fantasies that many women are inclined to project onto men.

If we include in the above list of theories (explaining the appeal that criminals have for women) the hypothesis that the longing to be violated requires a violator, then our model becomes more compelling, and some important principles become more tangible. We are now better able to understand why women make the choices they do - and why many women shun more civilized men. We obtain a better appreciation of Weininger's key insight that connects prostitution with criminality (where we interpret "prostitution" within the broader context of our own zeitgeist, namely, sexual permissiveness).

We might now infer how all these traits can be combined into a single "character" of evil manifested in female form. The woman who respects the violator will be attracted to the violator's deeds. She will consider civilized behavior boooooring and so loser. Hybristophilia will be a manifestation of her longing to be violated, but in the comfort of experiencing it from a distance, where she is instead aroused by the violation perpetrated on others.

**Towards cultural decay**

Let us remind ourselves of the appeal that bad-boys can have for women and why women make the choices they do... and how it relates to Weininger's key insight that connects sexual permissiveness with criminality. More specifically, why do women's choices matter, from a cultural perspective and why is it everyone's business? After all, if a woman chooses an idiot, is that not her problem alone? No, it isn't. It's our problem, and not just because we pay the taxes that go to support her thugspawn. A woman's choice in thug or criminal is her vote in favor of what she thinks all men should be. It is her contribution to cultural identity, what her culture stands for, and ultimately cultural decay.

# Domestic violence perpetrated by women

Study after study after study has shown that men and women perpetrate domestic violence at approximately equivalent rates, and yet the domestic violence bandwagon just keeps on rolling along. With Martin S. Fiebert's (2005)[51] extensive, annotated reference laying to rest any ambiguity as to the myths about domestic violence, it might seem incomprehensible how the domestic violence industry has gotten away with blaming men exclusively:

> SUMMARY: This bibliography examines 174 scholarly investigations: 138 empirical studies and 36 reviews and/or analyses, which demonstrate that women are as physically aggressive, or more aggressive, than men in their relationships with their spouses or male partners. The aggregate sample size in the reviewed studies exceeds 163,800.

The domestic violence controversy has been done to death, and the mainstream still just does not seem able to "get it." In the interests of completeness, however, Scott O. Lilienfeld and Hal Arkowitz (2010)[52] writing for Scientific American ask, "Are men the more belligerent sex?" They reference the oft-cited research of John Archer and Murray Straus, observing:

> Surprisingly, their analyses demonstrate that men and women exhibit roughly equal rates of violence within relationships; some studies hint that women's rates of physical aggression are slightly higher. This apparent equality is not solely a result of women fighting back, because it holds even for altercations that women start.

"Surprisingly?" Well, no it shouldn't be surprising at all, especially when we factor in the taboo that prohibits a man from ever hitting a woman, while a woman assaulting a man with rolling-pin or frying-pan has traditionally always provided the staple for hilarity, fun and family comedy. Indeed, a woman cutting off a man's penis and shredding it in the garbage disposal continues the tradition of familial hilarity in Sharon Osborne's nationally-televised 5-member CBS chat-show *The Talk*. It would seem self-evident where one sex is forbidden to ever hit the other while the other sex is encouraged to reflexively lash out on a whim that the actual patterns of domestic violence will be rather more complex than the simplistic bigger-is-badder myth favored by the mainstream. Of course, the well-established taboo that restrains men is not going to prevent all men from violent behavior against their partners, but it provides a major restraint that can easily offset the violence that is routinely encouraged in women against men.

# Setting the record straight on spouse abuse

## British crime survey self-completion questionnaire 1996

The objective of the British Crime Survey 1996 (Mirrlees-Black, 1999)[53] was to provide an accurate estimate of the extent of domestic violence in England and Wales, for men and women aged from 16 to 59. A Computer-Assisted Self-Interviewing questionnaire (CASI) was employed in order to increase respondents' willingness to report incidents by maximizing anonymity and confidentiality. Physical assaults and threats, as well as incidents that victims did not identify as "crimes," were also included in the questionnaire.

## Key findings

Of particular interest in this survey is the finding that:

> [...] the CASI method found relatively high levels of male victimisation, to the extent that men appear to be at equal risk to women of domestic assault (4.2% of both sexes reported an assault in the last year).

Among the victims of domestic violence, it was found that women were more likely to be injured (47%) than men (31%).

Women were far more likely to say that they had experienced domestic assault at some time in their lives (23% of women and 15% of men). While this observation does not seem to square very well with the finding that 4.2% of both sexes reported an assault in the last year, we see, nonetheless, that it certainly does square very well with the more popular message promulgated in the media, portraying women as victims and men as abusers.

Women were more likely to be chronic victims, where at least 12% of women and 5% of men had been assaulted on three or more occasions.

## Personal experiences of domestic violence

Interestingly, we see that male and female victims attributed different meanings to the assaults. "Virtually no male victims defined their experience as a crime, while only four in ten chronic female victims did so." Also, "the majority of female victims said they had been very frightened, compared to a minority of men."

Whatever we make of these figures, we can conclude that men's and women's *interpretations* of their experiences of domestic violence are very different, and that the popularized notion of female-only victimhood in the face of male-only perpetration is false. Importantly, if virtually no male victims defined their experience as a crime, we might expect that considerably fewer male victims than female victims will lodge formal complaints, This will impact on research findings that are based on statistical data. This concurs with another finding in the survey, where "incidents perceived as "crimes" were more likely to be reported to the police."

How men and women interpret their experiences of domestic violence is reflected in studies on relational aggression – for example, where Crick and Grotpeter (1995)[54] observed that schoolboys were more likely to implement overt aggression (among boys) because for them, the things that matter are "themes of instrumentality and physical dominance." Girls, on the other hand, were less likely to implement overt aggression. They favor relational aggression because for them, the things that matter most are relational issues during social interaction (e.g., establishing close, intimate connections with others). Hence, girls' attempts at harming others are more likely to be directed at relational themes, such as damaging or manipulating peer relationships, ostracizing others, spreading rumors, etc.

The British Crime Survey focused primarily on those incidents that would meet the legal definition of an assault (woundings, common assaults). Hence the survey is a measure of crime, and incidents that do not meet this definition, such a psychological abuse, were not analyzed in detail. However, we interpret the BCS figures on domestic violence, the all-important dimension of "relational aggression" was not included, and this presents us with an incomplete picture of domestic violence.

On the profile of domestic violence victims by sex (Chapter 4 of Mirrlees-Black's report), the survey observes:

> The degree to which men are victims of domestic violence is controversial. Some commentators claim that women are as violent as men in couple relationships (Lucal, 1995; Henman, 1996; Carrado et al, 1996). A more common view is that women are the main victims of domestic violence. It is argued that men commit assaults more frequently and more severely, and that women suffer greater direct and indirect consequences of such victimisation (e.g. Nazroo, 1995; Browne, 1993). Underpinning this view is the greater average physical strength of men and their more dominant role in sexual victimisation. Also, greater economic dependence and responsibility for children are factors that tend to make it more difficult for women than men to leave violent relationships.

As we've noted above, incidents of relational aggression were not considered in the BCS, hence a key dimension of domestic violence is missing.

Furthermore, women are *encouraged* to report incidents of domestic violence. They are *encouraged* to identify it, name it, and to not feel ashamed of themselves for reporting it. It is, indeed, relational aggression that the legal-political system is encouraging women to persist with; the often false reporting of physical aggression in men is the relational aggression that is the predisposition of women. Meanwhile, men are actively denied the very same consciousness-raising that is fed to women on a routine basis.

## Other research on the reality of domestic violence

The British Crime Survey 1996 is fairly conservative. Importantly, it ignores relational aggression. Nonetheless, the reality of domestic violence seems to be quite different to the generally accepted assumptions. We need not venture into elaborate explanations with respect to systems theory and semiotics after all (even though they are valid). There are many studies that do, in fact, show that women play an approximately equal role in perpetrating domestic violence.

Two major studies - Straus, Gelles and Steinmetz (1980)[55] and Straus and Gelles (1986)[56] - found that men and women assaulted each other at approximately equal rates.

Steinmetz (1981)[57] performed a cross-cultural analysis across six countries - Belize, Canada, Finland, Israel, Puerto Rico and the United States. For five of the countries, it was found that men and women assaulted each other at approximately equal rates, the only exception being Puerto Rico, where men were more violent.

In an analysis of data from almost 100 American and British studies, Archer (2000)[58] has found that women are more likely to initiate domestic violence against their partners than men and are more likely to be aggressive. While men are more likely to restrain themselves, when they do retaliate, they are much more likely to cause injury, and this is reflected in the study.

Like the BCS analysis, the above studies examine the domestic violence rates experienced by *both* sexes. This contrasts with feminist supported studies which are based in biased sampling, for example, questionnaires sampled from domestic violence shelters.

## Hard facts by way of actual convictions for murder

Statistics based on reports by agencies (such as police departments and hospitals) can be grossly misleading because of differences between men and women in their motivations to report incidents. For example, an aggressive marketing campaign directed at women to report domestic violence as opposed to the shaming of men who do report it. Propaganda tends to portray women as victims, men as perpetrators. Furthermore, for quite some considerable time women have been more likely to make false reports because of financial, legal or child custody inducements to do so.

Hard facts by way of actual convictions for murder are less likely to be manipulated along these lines, though we must also recognize the tendency of courts to be more lenient on women with respect to many such crimes.

In the United States, the Bureau of Justice statistics released a Special Report (1994) which detailed the results of a survey of family homicides in 33 urban counties. Referencing this report on their website, Reverends Sam and Bunny Sewell (2000)[59] observe:

- "In spouse murders, women represented 41 percent of killers."
- "In murders of their offspring, women predominated, accounting for 55 percent of killers."
- "Among black marital partners, wives were just about as likely to murder their husbands as husbands were to murder their wives: 47 percent of the victims of a spouse were husbands and 53 percent were wives."

From these figures, it is clear that:

- Men are *not* overwhelmingly the perpetrators of family violence;
- These homicide rates suggest that there is no basis upon which to presume that violence perpetrated by women will be "reactive" (and thus justified as a defensive reaction to violence).

## Violence by proxy

John the Other (2012)[60] provides an excellent critique on violence by proxy, and the reality that women get others, usually men, to do their dirty-work. He reminds us of Sally Fields' comment during her Oscar acceptance speech in 1980, "If Mothers Ruled the World There Would be No War." Again, like the whole patriarchal conspiracy agenda contrived under feminism, this idea is so ridiculous that the most appropriate response would be to laugh. But the fiction has sculpted reality, and the personal has become political. The ridiculous has morphed into law and it now denies us fundamental human rights. And so, we have a duty to state the obvious. Because it is so in-your-face obvious, we don't need to go into detail, and a point-form list will suffice:

- Women perpetrate violence by proxy when, through child abuse, they teach their children that violence counts, violence matters, and violence gets rewarded. Children first learn violence from their primary nurturer;

- Women perpetrate violence by proxy when they choose thugs, rapists and criminals. They do this because in their choices, they cast their votes in favor of the types of men that they think all men should be. In validating degenerate behavior, a woman becomes an accomplice in that behavior. Furthermore, women's choices are noticed by men. From women's choices and the kinds of behaviour that they validate, men learn what it is that most impresses women. They know what kind of behavior is to be emulated because they've witnessed the evidence that it works... though under the genocentric paradigm, particularly before Game (Chateau Heartiste, RooshV, etc) came onto the scene, many men had been rather slow on the uptake;

- Matriarchal subcultures are the source of violence when they raise thugs and expect their well-trained thugs to do their dirty-work. Irrespective of which part of the world you come from, many women choose thugs because, coming from the same abusive upbringing, thugs resonate with their own abusive natures. Like with like, and all that. But there is a further entitlement granted to an abusive woman when she chooses the company of violent thugs; they do her dirty work. Like that woman in Septa Philadelphia who phoned her accomplice thugs from the bus that she was on. They responded by arriving and shooting at the bus, after ushering her off, because another passenger criticised her abusive parenting skills. These are thugs who were likely raised by women. Usually raised by abusive women themselves, thugs know instinctively what's expected of them as men. Their womenfolk can direct proceedings from a safe distance without having to so much as lift a finger, and without having to confront the sorts of risks that they are exposed to. Such is often the nature of nurturing matriarchies – if momma ain't happy, ain't nobody happy. Tommy Sotomayor's (2013)[61] video, *Woman Calls Thugs To Shoot Up Bus After Argument With Passenger*, illustrates how this works;

- Anyone who fills up their car with petrol and buys plastic products is perpetrating violence by proxy because the oil-based resources that they consume become the oil-based resources over which wars are fought. And this complicity includes women. If, on the face of it, this example might seem obscure, it's not. It relates to systems theory as a crystallization of that famous aphorism, "what goes around comes around." It emphasizes how each of us is an accomplice in everything that is normal in culture;

- Women perpetrate violence by proxy when they vote for candidates who promise to support hateful, sexist and discriminatory policies such as VAWA and affirmative action;
- Women perpetrate violence by proxy when they make false allegations of rape;
- Women perpetrate violence by proxy when they pin white feathers onto the lapels of "cowards" who decline from fighting in their wars;
- Women perpetrate violence by proxy when they get their sons circumcised;
- Women perpetrate violence by proxy whenever they encourage someone else to be violent to another.

## Conclusion

There is no justification whatsoever for the feminist fantasy that men are more violent than women. This fantasy is pure projection on the part of feminists. Women are every bit as violent as men, and every bit as responsible for violence as men. There are no millennia of patriarchal oppression for which men owe women retribution. More likely, it is for the feminist nonsense of the past 50 years, and women's willing complicity in it, that women owe retribution to men.

# 3.3 THE WAGE GAP MYTH[62]

PREAMBLE: Being provided for is an important aspect of matriarchal power and authority. The wage gap myth has less to do with men oppressing women, and more to do with women's entitlements as the provided-for, nurturing sex. Contrary to what feminists would have us believe, hypergamous women have never been helpless victims subject to the wiles of opportunistic men, but astute decision-makers who have always been well-aware of their priorities and entitlements when choosing who should provide for them. Being provided for is an option that culture does not extend to men, and this impacts on the laws of supply and demand in the employment market and ultimately, the so-called "wage gap." Women are no less opportunistic today in the current climate where affirmative action grants them entitlement freebies that they've never had to earn on any level playing field. In both extremes, the wage gap, insofar as we might accept its existence as a given, has less to do with women being disadvantaged than it does with women enjoying the entitlements that have traditionally been extended to them in return for their responsibilities as primary nurturers.

In its original form, this topic was published as an article in the July/August edition (2004) of Transitions, by the National Coalition of Free Men.


A study in the May issue of *American Economic Review* (2003) had found that the wage gap between men and women was the result of lifestyle choices, and not discrimination. It was found that choice, not discrimination, is the determining factor in wage difference 97 percent of the time. The wage gap myth has been debunked numerous times -- for example, by the Independent Women's Forum, and the publication, "Women's Figures," by Furchtgott-Roth and Stolba (1999)[63].

The wage gap fiction was derived from the median wages of all men and all women in the work force, without regard to age, education, occupation, experience or working hours.

It's obvious, isn't it? You'd think that if you had to explain something so obvious, you might as well not bother and go and live in an ashram in India.

We know how it goes - women are likely to work fewer hours so that they can have more time to devote to the caring of children. Men are more likely to value career and therefore, work longer hours per day, devoting many more years to developing their expertise that makes them more valuable. Men are more likely to work in the death careers, such as mining (and therefore get paid more), whereas women are more likely to work in air-conditioned offices, regardless of their skill-level. Women are more likely to pull out of careers to raise a family; the stay-at-home mom is a legitimate, fulfilling option and an ideal escape-hatch. No such fulfilling option is extended to men. The man who chooses the stay-at-home option becomes an invisible drone, of no interest to men or women, employers or government, God or country. And so on.

The various studies that have been coming out have been equalizing the wage-gap disparities, and so feminists no longer have any basis to claim discrimination on the basis of sex.

As a further, more dramatic example, there was the *New York Times* article, *The Opt-Out Revolution*, by Lisa Belkin (2003)[64]. After arraying a formidable and damning indictment of a revolution choosing to opt out instead of persisting with the good fight, Belkin asks the rhetorical question, "Why don't women run the world?" Her answer is "Maybe it's because they don't want to."

Precisely. The wage gap is not a wage gap at all. It is a choices gap. Put simply, women have more choices than men. In most cases, their additional choices (e.g., stay-at-home-mom) require men to continue providing for them, and this is the reason for the wages gap.

Let's take a closer look at some of Belkin's observations.

- Stanford class of 1981 - 57% of mothers spent at least a year at home caring for their infant children in the first decade after graduation. One out of four have stayed home three or more years;
- Harvard Business School - In a survey of women from the classes of 1981, 1985 and 1991 it was found that only 38% were working full time;
- In surveys of professional women across the board - between one quarter and one third are out of the workforce, depending on the study and the profession;

- The United States Census shows that the number of children being cared for by stay-at-home moms has increased nearly 13% in less than a decade, while at the same time, the percentage of new mothers who go back to work fell from 59% in 1998 to 55% in 2000;

- Working mothers between the career-building ages of 25 to 44 - Two thirds of them work fewer than 40 hours per week (i.e., part time). Only 5% work 50 or more hours weekly;

- Compare these trends with those of men. 95% of white men with MBAs are working full time, while only 67% of women with MBAs are working full time;

- Belkin then turns her attention to the women in her Atlanta book club, and the roomful of women from Princeton University, "trained as well as any man. Of the 10 members, half are not working at all; one is in business with her husband; one works part time; two freelance; and the only one with a full-time job has no children."

- In a recent survey, the research firm Catalyst found that 26 percent of women at the cusp of the most senior levels of management don't want the promotion;

- *Fortune* magazine found that of the 108 women who have appeared on its list of the top 50 most powerful women over the years, at least 20 have chosen to leave their high-powered jobs, most voluntarily, for lives that are less intense and more fulfilling.

Perhaps the mechanism behind this trend can be explained in two words - escape hatch. Belkin quotes one of her interviewees: "I don't want to be famous; I don't want to conquer the world; I don't want that kind of life... Maternity provides an escape hatch that paternity does not. Having a baby provides a graceful and convenient exit."

Belkin refers to women social scientists who write about "how the workplace has failed women." And then she observes that "it is also that women are rejecting the workplace."

Closing off her article with a twist to her original question about women running the world, Belkin again asks why women don't run the world, and has one of her subjects answer it for her: "In a way," Amsbary says, "we really do."

Indeed. Women always have. Chivalrous, chauvinistic men (whose pro-feminism is a clever strategic move) believe that they wield the power -- the so-called "Frontman Fallacy." But in so many ways, they are deluded. Is a draft-horse pulling the cart more powerful than the driver wielding the whip? Does a guard dog patrolling the yard determine how its owner should live? How much power does a draft horse or a guard dog have over its own destiny? When a man dutifully and willingly subscribes to the provider role, he becomes a beast of burden whose first priority is to conform to the rules laid down not only by his employer but also by his wife and the social network that is her priority.

Belkin concludes her article with a positive spin, suggesting that "instead of women being forced to act like men, men are being freed to act like women... Looked at that way, this is not the failure of a revolution, but the start of a new one. It is about a door opened but a crack by women that could usher in a new environment for us all."

This is the basis of her message -- a new revolution for which women can claim the credit, that benefits both men and women.

While we would not wish to diminish the important and worthwhile goal of motherhood that must feature in every woman's life decisions at some point, what Belkin's article points to is a demonstration of the baselessness of the wage gap assumption. Hers is a most important admission that yes, many women -- even once they have attained their status as equals among men (albeit, with the helping hand of affirmative action) -- do not really want to work. Even with all the qualifications, skill bases and social connections that might make them heads of national corporations and leaders of nations, many women choose to throw it all in. Nothing wrong with that in principle, *except that every last woman in such a position has obtained her exulted status through affirmative action.* That is, through the assumption that, as a woman, she has the right to make her claim for the millennia of patriarchal oppression foisted against women by men. It's payback time. Payback for what?

Irrespective of what we make of Belkin's positive spin, we are left with very troubling questions.

What do we make of this collective arrogance? These career grrrls have decided that they've had enough, and then they continue to disparage men and men's achievements by suggesting that they might have a loftier purpose (motherhood). How insulting, to suggest that all this benefits men. These born-again moms are like occupying colonials trying to mollify the natives who have begun to show signs of becoming restless.

Whatever happened to the glass ceiling? Was it ever there to begin with? And now that progressive career grrrls have changed their minds, now that they realized that work was not all that it was cracked up to be, they white-wash it all with claims that everybody benefits, including men, because now men can be stay-at-home-dads if they want to.

All this might be well and good for some. But let us not forget the propaganda with which this new, purported vision was accomplished. Let us not forget the hatred that has been leveled against men and "The Patriarchy" in order to realize these goals. Now that we realize, with Belkin, that the wage gap is in fact a choices gap driven as much by women as by men, how do we justify the hatred and systemic biases that have been instituted against men over the past 40 years?

These career women that Belkin writes about (and among whom she includes herself) might as well have said "hey, we never meant it." Or perhaps, "lighten up guys, we were just joking." Or maybe, "it's a woman's prerogative to change her mind."

How do we interpret the past 40 years of feminist hatred against an entire gender -- men and boys, husbands and sons -- how is this justified? Why have so many women remained silent accomplices? Whatever happened to respect? This fabricated claim, that a glass ceiling had been instituted in some secret conspiracy by "The Patriarchy" to deny women opportunities in the workplace, is the basis for affirmative action. But Belkin's article further confirms that all this was a malicious lie -- a lie that denied the efforts and contributions that have always been made by men and a lie against which so few women have spoken out. Even now, it seems that Belkin is less speaking out against the lie than justifying the choices that she and others like her have made.

There never has been any such thing as a glass ceiling preventing women from getting ahead[*]. There has always been chivalry, placing

---

[*] Whatever it was that manifested as a glass ceiling was the result of joint complicity among men and women. That is, insofar as it can be argued that there were different salaries for the same work, for example, this salary differential was one of the many manifestations of the universality of the requirement - among both men and women - that women be provided for. The "ceiling" and its accompanying biases were as much the doing of women

the burden upon men to be provider, cannon fodder and all-round chump-horse doing the bidding of, entertaining and fulfilling women's every whim.

## Affirmative Action

In October 2001, following on from the terrorist attack on the twin towers in New York, the US Department of Justice announced that it was dropping its support of a sex discrimination lawsuit by women sitting for a test for Philadelphia's transit police, who claimed that it was unfair to female applicants. It took the event of September 11 to make everyone realize that there are some things (like carrying bodies up and down ladders) that women cannot do as well as men. In this light, Charlotte Allen, writing for the Independent Women's Forum (2003)[65], suggests that it took the terrorist attack on New York to put an end to the worst excesses of affirmative action -- meaning of course, affirmative action against men.

As far as Australia is concerned, affirmative action against men has been and continues to be enshrined in acts and legislation throughout the country, in the Equal Employment Opportunity for Women Act of 1999 (Affirmative Action) and the Sex Discrimination Act of 1984, for example.

Among the most "equal" and non-gender-specific of all these Australian (Commonwealth Government) EEO acts -- the Equal Employment Opportunity (Commonwealth Authorities) Act of 1987 -- also has to imply "reverse" discrimination in favor of women, with the following sections:

Section 3 (Interpretation) - program, in relation to a relevant authority, means an equal employment opportunity program designed to ensure that appropriate action is taken by the authority:
- to eliminate discrimination by it against;
- and to promote equal opportunity for; ... women and persons in designated groups in relation to employment matters.

---

as they were the doing of men. Among men, there was always an equivalent "glass barricade" that denied them entry into domestication and carer roles (such as stay-at-home husband, nurse or child-care worker).

In section 3 of the EEO Act where meanings are defined, "relevant" authorities must embrace equal opportunity programs that naturally favor women. Typically, no mention is made for equal opportunity for men. What does equal opportunity mean when only one side is invited? "Equal" suggests the participation of at least *two* parties and an impartial moderator. For the members of the one and only side that is invited, what are they supposed to be made equal to? Who does the moderating when there is only one party present? What is it that is being "moderated" when there is only one interest group to appease? Far from ensuring an unbiased platform moderating in the interests of a fair outcome between two parties, the EEO Act sounds to me more like women rule, men drool.

The essence and status of affirmative action, at least prior to the September 11 attack, was typified in the *Washington Post* article by Dan Froomkin (1998)[66], "Affirmative Action Under Attack":

> Affirmative action is the nation's most ambitious attempt to redress its long history of racial and sexual discrimination. But these days it seems to incite, rather than ease, the nation's internal divisions.
>
> An increasingly assertive opposition movement argues that the battle to guarantee equal rights for all citizens has been fought and won -- and that favoring members of one group over another simply goes against the American grain.
>
> But defenders of affirmative action say that the playing field is not level yet -- and that granting modest advantages to minorities and women is more than fair, given hundreds of years of discrimination that benefited whites and men.

Which brings us back to the wage gap myth and Belkin's article. As we've explored above:

- The wage gap has been thoroughly debunked and certified non-existent;
- Belkin's article above tells us how high-flying women with MBAs and law degrees flee their cherished careers because, well, it's just too hard, and women with more worthy priorities can do without the stress.

What does this all imply for the institutional bias against men, framed in the terms of Affirmative Action? If, as various sources confirm, wage differences have typically arisen from the choices that men and women made and not from discrimination, what is all this blather about women being discriminated against in the workplace by men? Redress for "hundreds of years of discrimination that benefited whites and men"? Indeed.

Yes, redress is indeed required. Men require redress for 40 years of feminist, hate-filled propaganda, vilification and harassment. Not all men, of course, because ultimately, chivalrous, powerful men continue to dominate the highest levels in the boardrooms, judiciary, industry and government, and they continue to do the bidding of feminists - as has always been the case even before modern feminism, when chivalrous men did the bidding of their womenfolk. It is the men lower down in the hierarchies - unskilled men, skilled and educated men, men of integrity, men who for whatever reason refuse to play by the contemptible rules - who require redress for an unprecedented and unjustified campaign directed against them over the past 40 years.

## Affirmative Action as Chivalry

It should become clear by now that affirmative action is just good, old-fashioned chivalry, pure and simple. Where before, we used to open car doors for the li'l ladies, presumably because they could not open car doors themselves, today we let them in front of us in the job queue, presumably because they cannot compete on their own merits.

## Male Suicide and the Emancipation of Women

The increase in men's suicide rates in recent times (the past 40 years or so) is a cause for concern the world over. From the Fathers for Life website (Schneider, 2004)[67]:

> The number of female suicide victims was considerably lower in 1996 than it was in 1979, in spite of a sizeable increase in the American population during that period. It declined from 6,950 to

5,905 annually. The number of the male suicide victims rose during the same period from 20,256 to 24,998 annually.

And:

> Extrapolating from those statistics to the early 1960s, when the impact of the new realities of no-fault divorce and the feminization of America became fully reflected in the escalating male suicide rates, and extrapolating to the year 2000, when its impact was still being felt to its full deadly extent, it can be estimated that a total of 800,000 American boys and men committed suicide in the 1962-2000 interval.
>
> In other words, more American boys and men died during and on account of the War of the Sexes than died in all military conflicts in which the USA was involved during the 20th century.

In Wendy McElroy's article in Fox News (2002)[68], "The Australian Institute of Health and Welfare (2000)[69] reports that the suicide rate for men aged 20 to 39 years has risen by 70 percent over the last two decades." With reference to Hoogland & Pieterse (2000) she also notes that "The Australian study's[70] suggested reasons for some of the suicides includes 'marriage breakdown.'"

Many studies on suicide (for example, Hoogland & Pieterse 2000[71]) suggest a particularly strong link between suicide and relationship breakdown. The conclusion being, perhaps simplistically, that relationship breakdown is the number one cause of suicide. Those of us who are more prone to thinking systemically (laterally), however, might conclude a "complex" of causes. For example, we now know that women initiate the majority of divorces, for such reasons as communication breakdown. Reading between the lines, in the absence of detailed research, what might the reasons be for "communication breakdown"? We can only guess. Though we might expect a promising candidate to be a man's employment status. "We've grown apart," or "I need to find my personal space," is Woman-speak for, "I've found someone else (a better provider, perhaps)," or, "You're too boring, dull and... unemployed."

What might be the connection between relationship breakdown and unemployment? In an article for the *Sydney Morning Herald* (Marginal Men, 10 October 1998), social commentator and sexologist, Bettina Arndt (1998)[72] writes:

These men [earning less than AU$15,600 pa] have been hit hard by the recent deterioration in the male labour market in Australia, which in the past 10 years has meant a 7 percent drop in full-time work. A striking 30 percent of men in their 30s are not in full-time employment. And now we have clear evidence that this recent dramatic drop in men's capacity to act as breadwinners means many are unable to maintain stable relationships.

Which then of course leads to the question - what's the connection that the affirmative action policies of the past 40 years have with unemployment rates and relationship breakdowns? And, subsequently, suicide rates.

Of course, other studies do implicate unemployment more directly as a factor. For example, it is widely recognized that suicide rates show a marked jump during periods of high unemployment, such as when it occurred during the 1930s.

All very messy and hypothetical, as systemic issues are notoriously difficult to resolve conclusively. As McElroy notes in her article[73], "yet, the motivation for male suicide remains a matter for speculation because little research has focused on the subject."

Suffice it to say that affirmative action, as one tool within the feminist arsenal of anti-male hatred, is built on a lie. Whether any study can establish conclusively a causal link between affirmative action and male suicide is secondary to the fact that feminism is a hate movement. Its premise grounded primarily in the wage gap has been proven as baseless, and its agenda directed at maintaining privileges for women by way of affirmative action is a con. We must conclude that women have never been systematically discriminated against in any patriarchal conspiracy perpetrated by men. Rather, men have maintained the tradition of chivalry, to provide for women, and this has exempted women from *having* to work. This escape hatch that is every woman's birthright is what is responsible for the wage gap.

Affirmative action and feminism are violations of the natural laws of supply and demand. They belong to a communistic ideology and their motivations are driven by envy and mediocrity.

In the past 40 years of feminist propaganda purporting discrimination, there has only ever been one group that has been systematically discriminated against -- and that is men. What sort of women's "emancipation" is this that only consolidates privileges for women, while denying men basic human rights?

## In Summary

- The wage gap myth is lethal. It is injurious to men's health. "More American boys and men died during and on account of the War of the Sexes than died in all military conflicts in which the USA were involved during the 20th century."
- For every woman alive today, irrespective of whether she is listed among the board of directors of a large company, or controls staff at middle management level, or sits at the reception desk of a small business, there is the inescapable perception that she has not earned her promotions. And the perception is real and justified.

Our first conclusion is a tragedy. But hey, men are expendable, so let's not give them a second thought.

Our second conclusion is also tragic. Because now, with the history of affirmative action, there is no grrrl alive who can convince us that she can do anything a man can do. Why is this a tragedy? Because there are genuine, capable women out there who do work hard, who are capable of meeting men on their own terms and who do deserve their promotions. But there is no way of identifying them. Their achievements will remain forever invisible, obscured by the cloud of affirmative action.

Feminists smugly trumpet that now that the tables have turned, men don't like it. Well, no, the tables have not turned. What has emerged is an entirely new situation, because we must conclude that women have not *earned* their power. It is this simple fact that makes the feminist phenomenon not a power reversal but the institution of a new kind of tyranny. At least when men were in power, everybody knew that, by and large, the power and influence was earned on a more-or-less competitive playing field. In *this* brave New World, however, we have something completely different, something far more insidious and destructive than a simple turning of tables. What has happened is the players have left the field and the spectators have taken their place. And instead of competition and winners we now have makeshift stalls and snake oil.

# 3.4 SEXIST WOMEN

In her chapter on "Woman's Sexism," Phyllis Chesler (2001)[74] does a fine job of exploring women's hostility to each other in ways that are sexist (biased against women). As she does throughout her important book, however, she occasionally reverts to an implicit assumption that women's sexism is reactive to men's sexism.

In her discussion on hostile sexism (HS) and its relationship to benevolent sexism (BS), Chesler focuses primarily on the work of Peter Glick and Susan Fiske (1996) and (1997)[75]. The work of Glick and Fiske provides us with an opportunity for analysis, because they make classic assumptions with respect to defining sexism (Woman good, man sexist). These sorts of assumptions are being made all the time. But Glick and Fiske's analysis, in putting themselves on the line with their more detailed analysis, within the context of HS and BS, puts a spotlight on the inherent flaws in the established assumptions regarding male sexism and female innocence-of-sexism. Their assumptions are complete nonsense, as we shall see.

*Glick and Fiske assume that men are the primary perpetrators of sexism, whereas the sexism of women is wholly reactive. There is no reason whatsoever to regard the sexism of women as reactive, secondary and contingent upon the sexism of men.*

Let us begin by defining some terms used by Glick and Fiske.

Hostile sexism is interpreted as sexism that objectifies women, treats women as incompetent and as property:

- Women are sex objects[*];
- Women cannot compete with men;
- Women control and manipulate men.

---

[*] No doubt it is an inconvenient truth for feminists that many women *like* being sex objects, and failing to be adulated as a sex object can often be a source of distress for many a woman.

Benevolent sexism is interpreted as sexism based on chivalrous attitudes. For example:

- Men should protect women and provide for them;
- "Ladies first." Opening car doors for them;
- Traditional assumptions about women - women as homemakers and nurturers.

From these two types of sexism, Glick and Fiske have derived the notion of "ambivalent sexism," which posits that sexism against women has a hostile component and a benevolent component. They suggest that women's complicity with benevolent sexism is the reward that women enjoy complying with men's hostile sexism. Notice the questioners' own implicit form of sexism, in that their questionnaire never even remotely considered sexism against men (that is, the sexism casting men in the provider role). The unspoken assumption is that men are the sole source of sexism.

## Woman's power of veto and "reactive" sexism

Before we proceed further, let us immediately dispense with the naïve implications inherent in this notion of women's sexism as inherently reactive to men's sexism (with its implication - Woman good, Man bad). First and foremost, it is widely understood that women are the gatekeepers of cultural norms. If women want to enter into a transaction where they enjoy the benefits of benevolent sexism in exchange for granting men the freedom to wallow unrestrained in hostile sexism, then it should be immediately apparent that women are not helpless victims, but rather, active participants exercising their formidable power of veto. Quite simply, men would not wallow unrestrained in hostile sexism if women did not allow them to. In their power of veto, women exercise their power of choice that makes it clear that they *like* their men as "hostile" sexists. In their choices, women cast their votes in favor of what they think all men should be. Whether or not one accepts that women's sexism is "reactive" to men's sexism, women's power of veto puts the responsibility for the choices they make, squarely in their laps. There is nothing "secondary" about women's complicity in sexism. Rather, their complicity is an expression of their most formidable power - their power of veto.

## Women's active sexism

Having dispensed with the notion that women's sexism is reactive and thus "secondary" to men's sexism, let us explore further, the real, active nature of women's sexism. The principle findings of Glick and Fiske are:

- Sexism (against women) is accepted by women nearly as often as it is by men - as men's sexism increased, so did women's acceptance of sexist traditions;
- Women's scores on benevolent sexism were on a par with those of men, and sometimes even higher;
- Women were more inclined than men to favour benevolent sexism over hostile sexism.

From our perspective, we are interested in the view of Glick and Fiske that "men's hostile sexism may free women to reject benevolent sexism as well as hostile sexism." Implicit in the view of Glick and Fiske is the clear assumption that sexism against women is ultimately the responsibility of men, and that women's sexism emerges as a response to sexist pressure from men[*]. Implicit is the notion that benevolent sexism "undermines" efforts by women to achieve equality by rewarding them for their complicity, thus defusing their resistance to patriarchal norms.

The assumptions and methodology of Glick and Fiske are deeply flawed. It all starts with the questionnaire, where sexism is assumed to be sexism against women. The notion that women are actively sexist against men has not even entered anyone's consciousness. Yet, for example, the culturally ingrained assumption - actively employed by women - that a man must be a provider before he can even be considered marriage material, is no less sexist than any of the hostile forms of sexism implied in their "ambivalent sexism inventory."

---

[*] But as we've seen, I can just as compellingly argue that the real power over sexism lies with women. They are the ones with the power of veto.

# Mutually assured sexism - provider object versus sex object

The role of Man as Provider is as integral to what is expected of men as having testicles. Rarely do women include in their list of required attributes that a man should have testicles. Similarly, the role of Man as Provider is the first condition that must be met before further consideration might be extended to a man's prospects as a marriage partner. The finer details of how rich he is, how he earns his income, his social connections and career aspirations provide women with the finer details that assist them in shopping for their ideal provider.

Thus, we know that women require men to be providers. It's the single constant, and it accounts for the variety of women's choices, where even a poor choice (a sensitive dishwasher) can be a good choice for a woman who eschews competition from her peers. (it is remarkable the compromises that women sometimes make in order to secure a provider who won't stray).

We have now accepted that the wages gap is actually a choices gap based in women's assumption that a man's primary responsibility is to provide for women. Women regarding men as money objects is no less sexist than men regarding women as sex objects.

Glick and Fiske categorize this requirement for the man to be the provider as "benevolent" sexism targeting women. Hello? How does *this* work? The notion that the requirement for men to play the provider role might be sexism is not on their map. Consistent with their solipsism, they phrase it as if it were a privilege that men are greedily indulging in their role as primary breadwinners, cavorting as happily in the workplace as sexist pigs in shit. To them, it seems that work is a hobby; work is something you do if you like, something you do if your fancy takes you. What are they projecting about the way that they view the world, and where they got their qualifications from?

We've seen previously how highly qualified women with MBAs and connections in high places take advantage of the stay-at-home-mom's escape hatch, to flee their cherished careers in favor of their stay-at-home options. Clearly, work is not the fun activity that Glick and Fiske have assumed it to be. Perhaps academics like Glick and

Fiske have a very different slant from the rest of us as to what constitutes working for a living.

Glick and Fiske are trying to tell us that if it favors women, then it is benevolent (manipulative) sexism, but if it favors men, it is hostile sexism. That's sexism, and Glick and Fiske are sexists. With their assumptions, hoisted by their own petard. QED.

## Provider object as chattel and canon fodder

A popular and persistent fable among feminists has been the notion of women as chattel. It is a reasonable guess that Glick and Fiske would probably share that view. But wait! Aren't men also regarded as chattel, in the same sense that we regard draft horses and guard dogs? Hillary Clinton seems to think so:

> Women have always been the primary victims of war. Women lose their husbands, their fathers, their sons in combat. Women often have to flee from the only homes they have ever known. Women are often the refugees from conflict and sometimes, more frequently in today's warfare, victims.

> First Lady Hillary Rodham Clinton
> First Ladies' conference on domestic violence
> San Salvador, El Salvador - November 17, 1998

Those guys dying on the battlefield, or returning home maimed and injured, just don't realize how lucky they are.

## Political correctness is sexism against women

In previous chapters, we've covered many examples of hostile sexism against men. Glick and Fiske demonstrate hostile sexism against men by basing their research questions on the assumption that all sexism is sexism against women. Furthermore, Glick and Fiske inadvertently reveal the extent of their entrenched sexism against women by rendering women's active sexism against men as irrelevant – women's sexism is harmless, while men's sexism has gravitas. They perpetuate the very assumptions that they are trying to quash, thus rendering women invisible! Cognitive dissonance much? You can't make this stuff up.

Do these researchers even know what sexism is? Contrary to their implied message and their agenda, women's views *do* count. Women's sexism against men *does* matter. Their sexism has gravitas because it consigns men to wars, it confines them to the provider treadmill, and it sends them to an earlier grave. Women's sexism against men is *not* more trivial than men's sexism against women.

In fact, we come to the *opposite* conclusion of Glick and Fiske. That is, rather than regarding the sexism of women as a response to men's sexism, it is more realistic to regard men's sexism as a response to women's sexism against men!

Ultimately, men who don't subscribe to the provider role don't count. They are invisible. When feminists take issue with the invisibility of women, the true invisibility of those most invisible - the bums and the homeless men that sleep in cardboard boxes or on park benches - cannot possibly rate a mention because they are considered not to exist.

## The power of women's sexism

We know the clichés:

- The hand that rocks the cradle is the hand that rules the world;
- Behind every powerful man is a strong woman;
- When Mama ain't happy, ain't nobody happy.

What might we infer about the pressures and expectations that mothers place on their boys, and that women place on their men? What might we infer about women's sexism towards men? Is Woman's role really "invisible", or is it the wellspring from which all cultural expectations - and sexism - emerge? Women are the managers, the networkers, and the strategists within the family groups. Men are their recruited agents. For all their alpha bravado, even the most successful men would not get past first base without the say-so of the matriarchal network that holds sway over our cultural norms. Displease the li'l lady, and he will likely have not only his in-laws on his back, but the rest of the network to which she has the greater access.

Men are the draft-horses and the guard-dogs doing Woman's bidding. When a man enters a woman's orbit, she restrains and controls his behavior with a leash that prevents him from going to extremes. Men are the embodiment and enaction of women's desires. By confining their range of vision solely to the bravado of alpha males, feminized culture has conned itself into believing that men are all-powerful, without understanding the matriarchal base from which that power springs.

Men must specialize their lives, whereas women are at liberty to leave their options open and to discover their more whole selves. Men must decide whether they want to be bricklayers, doctors, chefs, managers or engineers. And when men lock themselves into a choice (which they must do if they are to become successes and thus marriageable), then they pretty much confine themselves to options that must, by necessity, exclude most everything else.

Men are so busy specializing that they never have the time to conference on cultural directions. The success of feminism has been made possible because women, in being provided for, had the time to conference about their dissatisfaction with imagined oppressions. They worked themseves into a lather over it. With too much free time on their hands, they convinced one another that being provided for was a form of oppression. Men, who've had no such free time, never bothered to reply, never bothered to withdraw their provider services. They should have. Things might have turned out differently. But now, having passed Peak Clown at the previous turn, it might be too late. But I digress.

It makes much more sense to regard women's hostile sexism towards men (the sexism that treats with contempt those men that do not comply with the provider role) as providing the basis for men's ambivalent sexism towards women.

The myth of patriarchal sexism - portraying men as being eager participants in a systematic conspiracy directed against women - never had a shred of truth to it. If we wish to persist with the feminist-inspired myth that one gender alone "causes" sexism, then there can only be one answer - women were always the original sexists.

# Hypergamy and the utility of men

The truth about women as the original sexists is best understood in the context of hypergamy (defined in glossary). Hypergamy explains why women "marry up" and men "marry down," and that the worth of men is in their utility.

Men have utility as providers during times of peace and prosperity. They have utility as labor during times of poverty and adversity. They have utility as soldiers during times of conflict and war. They have utility as taxpayers in funding the state and its programs that favor women. They have utility as defendants in the family courts.

Women cannot help but see men within this context of utility, or usefulness. The utility of men as providers extends into their utility as agents acting in women's interests; hence, the utility of men in taking responsibility, defending and sacrificing in the interests of the provided-for.

A husband is a form of domestic appliance, like a toaster or refrigerator, and is just as expendable if it should outlive its usefulness. An industrious husppliance is a particularly valuable appliance that can magically repair broken devices, or replace worn out appliances with brand new ones. It can even mow the lawn, drive the car, pave the driveway, unblock drains, maintain bank accounts, pay bills and take the wife on holidays. Boston Dynamics, eat your heart out. To keep her husppliance in running order, a wife need do little more than cook and keep the house clean and dusted. Well, at least that's what it was like in the old days, before feminism.

These days, a woman can refuse to cook or keep the house clean, when she asserts her empowerment. If her husppliance becomes defective, she can replace it with another. Or if it becomes objectionable and refuses to function according to specs, then she can claim domestic violence, and seek redress through the family courts.

If it is not clear what role Glick and Fiske's references to benevolent and hostile sexism have to reality, by now, then let us set the record straight. Their obsession with sexism is projection of their own sexism, and that of the institutions that pay them.

Bottom line? The sexism in women's expectations of men is no less than the sexism invented in the feminist propaganda streaming from institutions and their gender studies programs. There are virtually no references in feminist literature to describe women's sexism against men, not because women are not sexist. Far from it. The reasons for their absence include:

- Their own sexism against men;
- Their ignorance of female nature;
- The failure of the dominant life-science (neo-Darwinian) paradigm.

And this brings us to the injustice that is affirmative action, seeking equality of outcome for men and women in the workplace. If men are raised to be providers and expected to be providers throughout their lives, then they will be more motivated than women, to focus on their careers. But feminists want to punish men for their higher motivation to compete and succeed. Equality of outcome, in the workplace, is bias in favor of women at the expense of men. Affirmative action for women is sexism against men. Women were always the original sexists, and feminists seeking advantages for women over men in the workplace is just another incarnation of women's Original Sexism.

# CHAPTER 4

# A MOST IMPORTANT EXPERIMENT

## An experiment that began 50 years ago

The most important experiment ever conducted began little more than half a century ago. We, the technologically advanced humans of the 21$^{st}$ century, are the lab-rats conducting experiments on ourselves, without any sense of the scale of what we have been playing with. Technology has impacted on our lives and the choices that we make to an extent that is unprecedented in human history. There's the internet and social media. More important, however, are the contraceptive technologies that have changed our biologies and the role of sexuality in culture.

Evolution is typically a long, slow process where incremental changes in phenotype might be detected over decades or centuries. With our contraceptive technologies, however, humans have rapidly accelerated the rate of evolutionary change, overturning the purpose of sexual relations in little more than half a century. This has had a dramatic impact on how men and women relate to one another. No longer is the purpose of sex about reproduction and survival. The script has been flipped completely. Sex is now principally about recreation and pleasure, and the commerce that promotes and profits from it. Reproduction is an almost incidental afterthought that can be terminated if the timing is inconvenient. Abortion has been integral to the realization of this new industry.

Our contraceptive technologies tamper with biology. They change the choices that become available to humans in culture. These are the choices that wire the neuroplastic brain. The implications of our contraceptive technologies have been profound and far-reaching, in ways that genocentric determinism can never account for.

Clearly, the choices to which we have been exposed over the past 50 years are unlike anything that has ever gone before. Renowned PUA Chateau Heartiste (CH) (2012)[1] would seem to agree, and makes his point with reference to an excerpt from paragraph 17 of the Encyclical Letter of his Holiness Pope Paul VI (1968)[2]:

> Not much experience is needed in order to know human weakness, and to understand that men -- especially the young, who are so vulnerable on this point -- have need of encouragement to be faithful to the moral law, so that they must not be offered some easy means of eluding its observance. It is also to be feared that the man, growing used to the employment of anti-conceptive practices, may finally lose respect for the woman and, no longer caring for her physical and psychological equilibrium, may come to the point of considering her as a mere instrument of selfish enjoyment, and no longer as his respected and beloved companion.
>
> (Pope Paul VI, 1968, p. 17)

CH makes the following significant observations:

- Just as contraceptives predispose men to devaluing women, so too, they predispose women to devaluing men - CH takes pains, however, to emphasize that it's *beta* men who are being devalued when women exercise their preferences for "risky sex with caddish alpha males on the make." As we shall soon see, CH's beta qualifier is problematic;

- CH guesstimates that his aggregate sexual experiences would have amounted to about one tenth of his actual record, were it not for the ready availability of reliable contraception.

CH's eminently sensible inference is that, in the absence of reliable contraception:

> A world in which women had to grapple with real, palpable fears of STDs, pregnancy and subsequent abandonment is, not to put too fine a point on it, a really shitty world for womanizers and serial monogamists and uncomplicated lovers of the art of seduction itself. I imagine I'd have to *gasp* start promising marriage or some such claptrap to any woman I wanted to bang, just to loosen her up enough to unhook her bra.

In other words, the ready availability of reliable contraceptive technologies throughout culture impacts directly on the choices that men and women make, and therefore, on how men's and women's brains are wired. That CH's sexual exploits would have been truncated by 90%, by his estimate, implies a serious variation in lifestyle attributable to the contraceptive pill.

Of course, CH's anecdotal opinion does not constitute the sort of empirical verification we require of falsifiable science. But what we are discussing is not amenable to traditional analytical methods because the subject matter has such serious implications. However, these questions do need to be addressed. We can't put them to the side while we wait for genocentric science to "catch up."

Let us review. By diminishing the inconvenience of ill-timed pregnancy to almost zero, the contraceptive technologies, with emphasis on the contraceptive pill and abortion, impacts on cultural logic principally in the following ways:

- Sex has been removed from its principle role relating to reproduction. Rather, it has become mainstreamed as a leisure activity, a form of entertainment, a commodity in a lucrative market catering to the laws of supply and demand, with outlets to cater to everyone's taste and convenience, from porn to prostitution. Our cultures' relentless immersion in a sea of pornographic images, online, on billboards, in newsagents, continues to remind men of their "needs," rewiring the brains of men who become ever-more convinced of the "needs" that are said, wrongly, to be programmed into their DNA. And it continues to rewire the brains of women who come to expect little of men beyond providing for their most basic utilitarian and reproductive interests;

- The impact on culture has been far-reaching and profound. And cultures wire our brains;

- A line has been crossed. What was previously forbidden in culture has become normal. New narratives and hierarchies have replaced the old ones. With new cultural benchmarks, peer pressure has replaced family values. Courage, honor and respect have been replaced by groupthink, opportunism and hate;

- New hierarchies of winners and losers have flipped the old scripts. What was irresponsible degeneracy in the old days has now become exciting, edgy and progressive;

- One might believe themselves to have escaped the flood of groupthink. But they are wrong, not only because cultures wire brains in subtle but profound ways, but also because life's opportunities, in careers, experiences and relationships, are impacted on by the toxic miasma that is in the air we breathe;

- The sexual revolution played a pivotal role in the rise of feminism. The emergence of feminism with our contraceptive industries was integral to our cultural transformation. Yet, the more that things change, the more they stay the same. Contemporary, feminist-inculcated culture remains fully gynocentric. Feminists seized the gynocentric narrative and mobilized chivalry and prostitution in new ways. Feminism is just old-fashioned chivalry reframed in the narrative of progressivism. Feminism pedestalizes women, and continues to rely on men to do women's bidding; the masquerade of women's empowerment in the workplace relies on men to be sacrificed in the interests of equal outcome. Like prostitution, feminism relies on chivalry to extract resources from men;

- On the abortion debate, celebrity atheists in support of abortion reasoned that in the old days, miscarriages and stillbirths were frequent. Thus they infer that abortion as the termination of life should be of little moral concern because, well, fetuses and newborns die. Moreover, we should count ourselves so lucky that thanks to abortion and our contraceptive technologies, women are spared the inconveniences of our ancestors. Maybe. But there's a crucial difference. Our ancestral mothers did not usually kill their fetuses or newborns as a matter of convenience. It takes a certain calculating mindset for a mother to kill her unborn with an attitude of indifference. It is a mindset that unifies the mother of the terminated fetus with the degenerate that fathered it;

- More to the point... it's not just that babies die, but it is their mothers who require them to be terminated.

If we have our reservations about religion, with its abstract, otherworldly references to impractical concepts like heaven and hell, then what we are witnessing today is the transformation of culture to a kind of hell on earth.

## In the absence of the constraints of childbirth

A TikTok conversation between a young man and woman, probably in their early twenties, maybe even younger:

HIM: How many guys have you slept with?
HER: Um no, I'm not saying.
HIM: Come on, I'm just, well, I really want to know.
HER: Nope, I don't want to tell you.
HIM: We're talking, like open and being honest. I won't get mad, I promise.
HER: Do you promise you won't get mad?
HIM: Promise, swear to god. How about we say our numbers at the same time?
HER: As in the count of three?
HIM: Yeah, count of three.

HER: Ok.
HIM: Ready, go…

| HIM | HER |
|---|---|
| 1… 2… 3 | 1… 2… 3 |
| 7 | 135 |
| Ummm… | 7… that's it?! |

HIM: Wait what?… excuse me... say that again... 135?!
HER: Well, yeah... I slept with a lot of guys...
HIM: Err, you sure did! 135??

He's surprised at her high count of 135. She's surprised at his low count of 7. One could almost detect a tone of disappointment in her voice at his unstudly notch count; accompanied by a thought bubble, "What am I doing with this loser?" What's going on here?

He's assuming that she inhabits the same world of scarcity that he experiences. She's assuming that he inhabits the same world of abundance that she experiences. Our contraceptive technologies have lifted all practical constraints from her world of options; meanwhile, he must now compete with the multitudes of spermatozoa vying for action. And both their rationalizations bear little resemblance to the reality.

These days in this era of fake news and social media, you don't believe everything that you see and hear on the internet, regardless of how convincing it might seem. The same goes for this TikTok scenario outlined above… why would anyone subscribe to a private conversation such as this while being videoed? But it doesn't matter. It's a scenario that we can imagine playing out in real life; and often, also in the opposite direction (woman with low count, man with high). Regardless, this is a realistic scenario that serves the point that I want to make.

In order to obtain any action in the bedroom, the onus is always on the man to initiate. He must switch himself into "on" mode. To score with women who are selective, he is required to do the performance routine; be funny, provide the witty repartee that shows that he's on top of his game, demonstrate social proof. To score with women who are less selective, he needs to play the numbers game and roll his dice.

Either way, the onus is always on the man to initiate. He has to want it. He has to be motivated to do the Silly Dance. In comparison with other men, however, for the PUA, there is one nuance that is especially critical; he has to want it, while masquerading an alpha veneer of sexual indifference.

If a man is not motivated enough, if he puts in only a partial effort, he is much less likely to be successful. This applies even if he's attractive to women, because the onus is always on him to make it work; women lose interest if they have to do any of the spadework, because they question whether he's really interested. The onus is always on the spermatozoon to demonstrate interest. Of course it is. No interest; no boner; no action.

For a woman to obtain any bedroom action, she must first don her disguise (cosmetics, perfume, hair, fashion) to transform her drab 6 or 7 into the hot 9 or 10 that PUAs notice. With that out of the way, the rest, for her, is easy. She has only to:

1)  Turn up;
2)  Play along with his script;
3)  Submit.

If she doesn't like his moves, she monkey-branches to someone else who will jump through all the hoops to impress her, for the self-esteem of considering himself an alpha with a healthy notch count.

## Novelty and excitement amid a sea of mediocrity

If we accept the thesis that central to female sexual arousal is the thrill of the forbidden (meaning the cultural forbidden, where it is culture that establishes what is known and permissible about the world), then whence do women have this need met? Can a PUA performing tricks like a circus monkey, or an aging rock legend, or any other uber-alpha tallying hundreds of paramours or more, make a woman feel like she's doing something novel, exciting and forbidden? What happens when the forbidden becomes mundane?

Perhaps one solution to the modern woman's impending disappointment is not an uber-alpha with the predictable grind of innumerable encounters, but an uber-thug, predisposed to unpredictable mood swings and violence. Much has been written about women's attraction to dangerous criminals and rapists who have been convicted. The word to describe this proclivity is *hybristophilia.*

Julie Bindel's (2012)[3] thesis is that the women who fall for convicted criminals are, contrary to media portrayals of them as unhinged, "... well adjusted, with good social skills." Among her examples, she cites the story of "bright, articulate and immediately likeable" socialite Rosalie, who had gone on from her marriage to socialite lawyer Victor Martinez, to marry convicted rapist and serial killer of women, Oscar Bolin. A contrasting turn of events to say the least, given that in her second marriage, any thought of throwing parties for politicians and celebrities was no longer available.

Bindel quotes from her conversation with Dr Lorraine Sheridan, a forensic psychologist with the Sellenger Centre for Research in Law, Justice and Social Change at Australia's Edith Cowan University:

> Women who get into relationships with death row prisoners often have much in common with those who spend their lives creating shrines to and writing to celebrities [...] These women have a relationship, in their perception, with an exciting, high-status person [...] The death row romances take this a step further, in that they are able to have a reciprocal 'celebrity' relationship. There's also the factor of having nabbed an ultra alpha male, one who has carried out the greatest of violent acts.

At one level, all this seems to corroborate the alpha/beta dichotomy that the PUA community takes for granted. But at another level, there seems to be something missing from this picture. The incarcerated criminal of Rosalie's second marriage is not strutting about like a conquering alpha. Rather, he is rotting in a cell, his spirit bowed and subdued. Psychically, he must surely be decimated, and his wife would seem to have him right where she wants him, under her control in a prison cell – writes Bindel:

> Yet there is something grotesque about the way they objectify these men in cages and are able to exercise absolute control over them.

Who would have thought? Is there something about our zeitgeist that is leaving women somehow unfulfilled? One thing we can say for certain... Rosalie's incarcerated alpha Oscar Bolin is no dandy Giacomo Casanova.

From a broader perspective, our inferences are consistent with those of Otto Weininger (1906)[4], who observed a relationship between criminality and prostitution. The shared principle being that there is something about female sexuality that in moral conduct is drawn to the formidable and the possible in man, but in immoral conduct is drawn to the dangerous and the degenerate. The thrill of the forbidden is related to the thrill of throwing it away.

## Criminality and prostitution

Weininger's reference to the relationship between criminality and prostitution is an important one that points to a fundamental relationship between male and female sexuality. What is it about criminality that draws prostitution into its orbit? It is exactly the same thing that relates to contemporary women's fascination with bad boys. Women of the feminist era are drawn to the alpha stereotypes that mock traditional patriarchal roles. They are persuaded by the alpha masquerade of dominance. They are active participants in the bully-victim dynamic that respects the thug and regards with disdain the loser that declines from asserting his will.

The personal testimonies in *Prostitution Narratives: Stories of survival in the sex trade* (Norma & Tankard Reist, 2016) provide invaluable insights into the enormous harm that prostitution and other forms of sex work does to women, but none of them provided the answers that I was seeking. What I wanted to know, from a woman's perspective, what it was that draws women into such obviously harmful lifestyle choices. I've come to the conclusion that the editors themselves don't know. More specifically, they *cannot* know because they are women, and they will encounter their experiences from within a woman's deeply immersed perspective. If you asked a talking fish to tell you about water, it won't be able to, because it has no conceptualization for not-water. Same thing with women in the sex industry, they are too immersed in it, with their priorities and their rationalizations, to properly understand the dynamics of how they got there. And so, we need to work through this ourselves. Here's my take, for what it's worth.

As we've established in earlier chapters, women, at a primal level, are drawn to the formidable in man. They are drawn to the formidable in men because they yearn for connection with something larger than themselves. They seek liberation from conformity, girly social networks, gossip and mediocrity. They want access to the cleverer, smarter, bolder, more dominant. They are drawn to possibility and to mystery, the mystery of the unknown. They are drawn to that which excites them, maybe even scares them. The thrill of the forbidden is the thrill of submission. And taken to its logical conclusion, the thrill of submission can become the thrill of throwing it away. Rape fantasies and all that.

Women crave validation from men, and so they are drawn to men who they can look up to. Women look to men for direction. It's a replay of the old, familiar narrative which assumes that men lead and women follow; in everything from marriage, work and family, to dance, conversation and sex. Men initiate, and women accept or veto. This is as true today as it was in our grandparents' era. Feminism, however, has obscured it from view because feminists deny the truth about female sexuality. An extension of this narrative is the notion that women need to be saved. Saved from what? From men? From themselves? From their sexuality?

Some girls from traditionally conservative or religious backgrounds might question their moral upbringing and look for answers by dabbling in lifestyles that invariably lead them into the sex industry. Their craving for validation from men predisposes them to submission to the will of men. Among these men are the opportunists, drug-addicts and predators of the big cities that young, naïve women might be visiting for the first time. Their naiveté predisposes them to being taken advantage of by men. As they immerse themselves into prostitution culture, they become groomed by it, and establish their expectations around it. Those who willingly remain immersed within that way of life may rationalize, and thus believe, that they have no regrets. But for the minority that do wake up one morning and realize the horror of what they've done, the realization can be traumatic. And to their way of thinking, they can't undo it.

So why do good women make stupid choices? An important part of contemporary culture is the progressive narrative playing out in tandem with the dominance narrative. A promiscuous woman thinks herself progressive and liberated, and the dominance narrative continues to play into her craving for validation. Pretend-alphas are able to masquerade a dominance that women are easily impressed by. They lead, women follow. In earlier times, emotionally stunted adolescents, trying to assert their place in the pecking order, would have been unable to get away with this kind of masquerade because older narratives, with their emphasis on "old-fashioned" (patriarchal) values, were more difficult to contrive. Today's paper-alpha masquerade, however, provides for men the sort of camouflage that cosmetics provide for women... both play nicely into our shallow culture with its emphasis on appearances and first impressions.

Another problem that many women face is that women learn what men are like from the types of men that hit on them. If they are constantly being approached by a certain type of man, then that is what they will assume all men to be. They never get to discover the kind of man that is comfortable in his own skin. Women so exposed quickly learn to expect little of men, and for many of them, a life in prostitution becomes a valid lifestyle choice. The young woman seeking adventure in a new city is particularly at risk, where the onus is on her to set about making new friends and to explore *and discover* new lifestyle options.

Here we encounter that problem with determinism, again. It is the distinction between instinct versus free will, immutable facts versus dynamic discovery. Nobody is "wired" with facts about the world. With neuroplastic brains, people are primed for discovering the world, and the young woman encountering a new city has to discover for herself its treasures and its traps.

Notice how, within the context of the gamete model of social engagement, the kinds of problems that women face cannot apply to men. Men are interesting to women in many ways, but the problem of being bombarded by female strangers is one that only celebrities might, in their artificially contrived atmospheres, enjoy. Or, to put it another way, it is because women have it so easy that they have it so hard. Denied the challenges that routinely test and harden men, women remain vulnerable to being taken advantage of. The sperm-egg dynamic that plays out at the level of the gamete intrudes into social life in culture, and there is no possibility of circumventing it.

Many women get into prostitution because they are lured by the promise of bright lights, glamour, excitement and attention from men. Some of the testimonies (Norma & Tankard Reist) confirm as much. Other testimonies describe women who get into prostitution because they have been groomed and trafficked from one abusive context to another. These are also important, but they are much more difficult to unpack within the confines and purpose of this small book.

The position of Norma & Tankard Reist is distinctly feminist. Though they believe that prostitution is bad for women, as feminists, they blame The Patriarchy... women good, men bad. They don't understand men *or* women, and the importance of the matriarchal role in culture. True to form, they believe that feminism is good for women, it liberates women, women can do whatever men can do, women can be as good as men. And women can be as bad as men (and not have to apologize for it). They haven't a clue. They don't see how they've *disempowered* women.

Feminism denies women their power of veto, it disempowers women and deprives women of the confidence and agency to say no. Feminism, like the neo-Darwinian biology that informs its unarticulated assumptions, has been an unprecedented disaster.

So, in closing, let us re-iterate one more time, because it is so important: Neo-Darwinism, with all the technologies, artifacts, values and assumptions that have spawned under its dogmatic scientism, has been an unmitigated disaster for our cultures and the lives ruined under its pervasive influence.

# CHAPTER 5

# IT'S THE MATRIARCHY, STOOPID

We, the ingesters of the red pill, are now well familiar with the extent of lying and deceit by feminists. Here we provide further examples to place emphasis on the intercultural aspects of that deceit, and how it amounts to a form of cultural interference that has much in common with the Christian crusades. Further, by going intercultural, we might obtain a greater appreciation of the patriarchy-matriarchy duality that is integral to all cultures, universally.

## Boys and men just don't matter

In his Huffington Post article *1 In 9 Girls Marries Before Age 15, And Here's What Happens To Them*, Diehm (2013)[1] writes:

> December 10 marks the anniversary of the presentation of the United Nations' Universal Declaration of Human Rights, which recognizes that there are "equal and inalienable rights of all members of the human family." But, because of the widespread practice of child marriage, 14 million girls under 18 are denied those rights each year. Here are some facts about the lives of child brides…

The article then trots out the predictable maps and graphics showing that 14 million girls are married every year before their $18^{th}$ birthday. Girls' death before childbirth and low education of girls and poverty proves all-round global mayhem directed at girls, presumably, by The Patriarchy.

No mention of boys. We have no idea what boys experience. Are boys better off? Or are they worse off? Clearly, neither Diehm nor her employer (Huffington Post) is interested in this question.

Now factor in Stephen Komotho's letter to Mike Buchanan (2013)[2] where he, as a Kenyan, brings to light the boys' perspective of life as Masai warriors and child laborers. In other words, in cultures where girls are frequently removed from school to be forced into marriage to much older men, boys are also removed from schools early to be pitted against wild animals and warriors from hostile tribes, and to learn about protecting and providing for families. Many young girls removed from school early get married... some die in early childbirth. Many young boys removed from school early become hunters and "morans" (warriors)... some die early in the heat of survival. I'm not too sure which of these parties has the rawer deal, but most of us would realize that the patriarchal privilege of fending off lions and tribal warriors is unlikely to be the barrel of entitled laughs that feminists would seem to presume it to be.

Writing for Slate.com, citing the culling of men in war-torn Chechnya as an example, *Harford* (2006)[3] provides a more realistic outline of the relationship between the patriarchal privilege of dying prematurely and how this impacts on women's marital prospects.

[SIDENOTE: At this point, after googling around on the internet, it has been difficult to track down any reliable research establishing a consistent relationship between *polygyny* (Wikipedia, 2014)[4] and the casualty rates of men compared to women. Anecdotally, historical evidence suggests a relationship between polygyny and heavy war casualties among men resulting in a surplus of women available for marriage. In the context of contemporary African tribes, how might different cultural pressures on men and women play out in the patterns of polygyny, polyandry and polygamy? These are non-trivial questions that cannot just be glossed over to further a sexist feminist agenda.]

Developed and developing countries (2$^{nd}$ and 3$^{rd}$ world) are especially vulnerable to being overtaken by the feminist propaganda machine unopposed. For example, we see a similar pattern taking place in Iran, where the purported plight of women in divorce, without any reference to how divorcing men are treated, serves to promote the feminist agenda unopposed, of a world-wide conspiracy against women. Happily, we have Ali Mehraspand (2013)[5], who set the record straight on the true nature of divorce in Iran.

This scale of idiocy has been ongoing for the best part of 50 years. It doesn't matter where you look. If it's a publication peddling *The Patriarchy Oppresses Women* agenda, you can rest assured that it will cherry-pick only those aspects that they can construe as "oppression" of women while omitting those aspects that prove the opposite. Pick your topic. Wage gap. Domestic abuse. Sexual assault. Doesn't matter.

## Women doing it to women

Previously I referenced Chapter 6 of Jomo Kenyatta's book (1965), showing that FGM is *female* surgeons performing the clitoridectomy, and *female* sponsors and villagers participating in the celebrations. As per Kenyatta's example, FGM is a girl's rite of passage into adulthood. Let us explore the implications further, to show how politicized the issue has become, in the interests of the feminist industry.

For feminists, the equation is as simple as 1+1=2. Female genital mutilation (FGM) = patriarchy = rape culture. Except for one teency weency little problem. *It has always been women doing it to women.*

On their Fact sheet No2 41, the *World Health Organization* (2013)[6] regurgitates the predictable rhetoric linking female genital mutilation (FGM) to... you guessed it... The Patriarchy:

FGM is recognized internationally as a violation of the human rights of girls and women. It reflects deep-rooted inequality between the sexes, and constitutes an extreme form of discrimination against women.

Writing for the Huffington Post, *Hilary Burrage* (2013)[7] launches The Feminist Statement on FGM beginning with the opening premise:

> The basic premise of our statement is this:
>     Patriarchal oppression is the bedrock of female genital mutilation (FGM) and related harmful traditional practices... female genital mutilation (FGM) in all its forms is cruelty and abuse.

Under her subheading *Powerful invisible interests*, you begin to suspect that sunlight is beginning to penetrate into the dankest, densest, darkest recesses of her atrophied brain, when she acknowledges that "... some of those who benefit are the grandes dames of the mutilating communities - the secret Sande Society women who control or perpetrate the torture." But just as you begin to suspect that Burrage might be capable of at least some semblance of a snail's level of rational thought, out trots the predictable patriarchal conspiracy theory:

> But always behind them stand the shadowy men who pull the real strings: the men who prefer child brides, the men who sell their barely teenage daughters, freshly mutilated, into marital slavery, the men who decree, perhaps via their womenfolk, that 'unclean' (uncircumcised) women are unfit to be members of the community.

The reality, however, does not sit so comfortably with the *it's-the-Patriarchy-Stoopid* narrative. You will likely see the same pattern of FGM pretty much wherever you look. It's women doing it to girls. At no stage in my research on FGM have I found a single reference suggesting that it was a man or cabal of men forcing FGM on women or girls. In the strictest terms, FGM appears to be "women's business", a women's-only sacred ritual, generally, where neither men nor boys are invited. In a very real sense, FGM appears to be a *celebration* of what it means to be a woman (this is not to condone it; such practices are problematic, but let us call it for what it is... FGM is not intentional abuse but another culture's form of celebration). As a celebration of tribal girls' rites of passage into adulthood, FGM is part of a ceremonial process to which men are neither invited nor wanted (boys and men celebrate their own rites of passage). There might be exceptions, but I have never found any.

In the meantime, feminists' interference in the traditions of cultures that they know nothing about amounts to an especially toxic kind of cultural interference, especially when you factor in the *forced circumcision campaigns in Africa* (O'Hara, 2013)[8]... some of us might be reminded of the Christian crusades and the cultural interference that had established their credentials.

What part of *"women doing it to women"* do feminists not understand?

## The other dimension of oppression

The irony is that in feminists' obsession with The Patriarchy, there exists a whole other class of oppressors that is getting away with murder. Which brings us to the *relational aggression* (Wikipedia, 2013)[9] that we discussed previously. This is the reality of the oppression of women by women and the nature of matriarchal authority. Phyllis Chesler's (2009)[10] *Woman's Inhumanity to Woman* provides insights suggesting that women cannot count on support from women just because they are women, and the childish tendency of feminists to regard all women as friends just because they are women suggests an emotionally stunted view of the world.

With their tendency to project their infantile view of the world, we should expect feminists to reduce any discussion of the relationship between patriarchy and matriarchy to a competition of meanness and who is the bigger bully. The truth is much more complex than the victim narrative that constitutes feminist discourse.

## Conclusion

Patriarchy is one important dimension of the *complex system* (Wikipedia, 2013)[11] that is culture. The other crucial dimension, the one rendered invisible by feminists, the one first teaching children about hypergamy, gender roles, relational aggression, violence, genital mutilation and all the rest, along with the importance of compliance with said cultural norms, is Matriarchy.

# CHAPTER 6

# EQUALITY WITH ESCAPE HATCH IS NOT EQUALITY

TRIGGER WARNING FOR FEMINISTS: ANY REFERENCE IN THIS SECTION TO THE STERILIZATION OF GIRLS IS SATIRE, AND IS INTENDED ONLY FOR ILLUSTRATION PURPOSES. THE AUTHOR IN NO WAY ADVOCATES ANY SUCH ACTION.

We live by narratives. Narratives are contexts that are best understood as strings of logic. The narratives of providers are very different to those provided for. The presence of an escape hatch makes all the difference in how women view the world.

> *No woman should be authorised to stay at home to bring up her children. Society should be totally different. Women should not have that choice, precisely because if there is such a choice, too many women will make that one.*

Simone de Beauvoir, in Friedan, (1976) –
"A Dialogue with Simone de Beauvoir"[1]

The other day as I was walking in the sunshine, pedestrians suffered the inconvenience of having to step off the footpath and onto the road because a team of sweaty, singlet-clad men with dirt and dust sticking to their sweat were digging a trench. Shoveling spades of dirt alongside the trench with the precision of surgeons wielding scalpels, there was hardly any dust wafting into the path of pedestrians. They were all men of course, and I could confidently conclude that they weren't digging the trench for the joy of it. Between the trench and the road, a number of well-dressed women holding designer handbags in their manicured hands were waiting at the bus-stop, scowling at having to contend with the little bit of wind-blown dust that our spade-wielding surgeons could not avoid. Oh, the inconvenience. I wish I had a camera. There could be no more compelling example of the dynamic between slave and entitled. No doubt, some of the women were off to work in jobs that they would not be in were it not for Affirmative Action policies, to account for all those millennia of oppression of women by men. So, what was the likelihood that any of the women standing at the bus stop would trade places with any of the men digging the trench?

## A natural law of the universe

Simone de Beauvoir understood the nature of the problem. Her comment to Betty Friedan, above, while made from a woman's perspective, was ultimately an expression of a fundamental law for all life throughout the universe. Namely, every living organism is inclined to choose the path of least resistance, least pain, greatest reward. All organisms are pain-averse and reward-seeking. If they weren't, they would die and life itself would not be possible. Neither ecosystems nor free markets can exist without this principle. In a free market, between two items identical in every way but bearing different price-tags, a sane person will always choose the cheaper.

Likewise, consider choosing between a life committing to a STEM trajectory that typically promises high stress, long hours and working in a demanding environment versus staying in a comfortable home and being provided for by someone else who is committed to said high-stress, high-performance treadmill. To someone for whom both options are culturally sanctioned, the preferred choice should be obvious. The options become even more pronounced when said provider is a miner or construction worker. No woman needs to be oppressed by any patriarchy, nor anyone else for that matter, to choose the most comfortable option. The great law of the universe cuts across all living organisms, all persons across all cultures, all lifestyles, and both sexes. Women instinctively realize where the better deal lies. No women's studies major is required to understand this, though if they must; Simone de Beauvoir.

It is often difficult to see how the other side experiences their world. While we might expect that some women will perceive the grass to be greener on the provider side, a free market based on equal opportunity will test a woman's resolve and the question will, with a bit of serious introspection, be laid to rest. It must also be said that the questions are not always unreasonable. Old-boy networks have their own history of privilege and entitlement, and challenging these is to the benefit of both men and women. But these kinds of questions have little part to play in the contemporary feminist agenda.

## Escape hatch changes perceived risk and motivation

So how do we resolve the issue of gender inequality in the workplace? The only way to approximate true gender equality in the workplace is to remove the stay-at-home option that is available to women. Exactly as Beauvoir suggests. The question is, how do we accomplish this in any meaningful way?

Beauvoir understood that women are raised in this world with an escape hatch. This ever-present soft option wires women's brains, and relates to the topic of neural plasticity, and *how experience changes the brain* (Cherry, n.d.)[2]. For example, Haier et al (2005)[3] found that men's and women's brains differ in the distribution of white (glial) and grey (neural) matter, with intelligence tests showing that on average, men used 6.5 times as much grey matter as women did, but that women used 9 times as much white matter as men did. Soft and hard options wire brains differently.

Women have permission to leave if the going gets too tough, or even to not consider going there if it looks too much like hard work. The reason that so few women do STEM courses is that they don't have to. It's the reason why so few women work in mines or construction sites, or sweep roads or dig trenches – they don't have to. This has nothing to do with Patriarchy oppressing women. What woman would choose to work in demanding, stressful situations, or dirty, life-threatening situations if they didn't have to? Does one really need a women's studies degree to answer this question?

And once we realize that stay-at-home women don't work because they don't have to, a whole slew of other don't-have-tos falls neatly into place. For example:

- Women don't rob banks because they don't have to;
- Women don't get into violent confrontations because they don't have to;
- Women don't pursue stressful career paths because they don't have to;
- Women don't pursue dangerous career paths because they don't have to;
- Women don't pay for their share of the expenses on a date because they don't have to;
- Women are less likely than men to be homeless because they don't have to (provide for themselves);
- Women are less likely to be imprisoned because they don't have to (take the same risks as men);
- Women don't fight in wars because, you guessed it, they don't have to.

These are all different ways of saying *pussy-pass*. Of course "because they don't have to" comes with subtexts. For example, "because they have men doing it for them" or "because they can":

- Women work in air-conditioned offices instead of dusty, dangerous mines because they can;
- Women stay at home because they can;
- Women (prostitutes) accept payment for selling their bodies because they can;
- Women rely on men to take the initiative because they can;
- Women rely on men to do the heavy lifting because they can;
- Women cry because they can;
- Women play the helpless victim because they can;
- Women have a rationalization hamster because they can.

Nobody is being oppressed. Women do these things because they can.

The sub-texts that women enjoy as entitlements become the subtexts that men actualize as obligations:

- Men work because they must (they have no choice);
- Men work in dusty, dangerous mines instead of air-conditioned offices because they must (nobody is going to provide for them);
- Men pursue stressful career paths because they must (they know what has to be done to secure their place in the hierarchy);
- Men pursue dangerous career paths because they must (they know that a provider raising a family has responsibilities);
- Men get into violent confrontations because they must (sometimes their survival depends on it, and sometimes wars require it);
- Men pay the expenses on a date because they must (it's just what providers do, and women will look elsewhere if said date does not deliver on his obligations);
- Men pay for sex because they desire (men are never desired for anything other than what they can provide);
- Men take the initiative because they must (they would finish up with nothing if they did not);
- Men do the heavy lifting because they must (they would receive no reward if they did not);
- Men don't play the helpless victim because they must not (they receive no reward for it other than a cardboard box and homelessness);
- Men don't have a rationalization hamster because they don't have that luxury (their assumptions are constantly being tested and revised in accordance with the penalties exacted for wrong choices).

Let us take a closer look at this *rationalization hamster* (Urban Dictionary, 2012)[4] phenomenon, because it kind of wraps up our point about the relationship between experience and character, and how this relates directly to *how brains are wired* (Wikipedia, 2014)[5].

Women's solipsism and impulsiveness rely on the fact that they don't need to have their perspective of the world tested. Their rationalization hamster is at liberty to scamper hither and thither, rarely having to contend with consequences or having to take responsibility for bad choices. Again, it is their ever-present soft option... the option to stay at home... that colors their risks and becomes habituated and wires their brains.

This is all another way of expressing the point made in *Alison Tieman's* (2014)[6] video describing gender roles in the context of actor and acted upon. When we talk about equality in the workplace, we are talking about changing the relationship between actor and acted upon... we are ultimately talking about changing biology.

Beauvoir's observation makes perfect sense. But where her reasoning falls down is in the assumption that you can somehow manipulate women's motivations through propaganda and the force of law. Nothing could be farther from the truth, because the mere availability of the soft option, whether or not it is taken, colors *all* choices and the risks associated with them. The same option, to a woman or a man, is the difference between *suck-it-and-see* and *do-or-die*. A woman can entertain the idea of being a fire fighter as a dare, maybe for a joke or for a laugh, and affirmative action will enable her to actualize her whimsical flight-of-fancy. She is at liberty to *suck-it-and-see* and then have a laugh if it does not work out. A fire fighter, by contrast, is unlikely to perceive his role in quite the same way. For him, it's a career choice, an identity, a way of life, a statement of something that he stands for.

## The solution

The only solution that might bring us in any meaningful way closer to true equality in the workplace is to close the escape hatch; bolt it down, lock it up and throw away the key. More specifically, permanently sterilize all females before they reach reproductive age. Only this step can stand any realistic chance of removing the stay-at-home option from women's choices. Only this step might make redundant the primary nurturer role that justifies the stay-at-home option for women. Only this step can stand any chance of rewiring the brains of men and women to make women more competitive with men in the workplace. Why? Because it is the only way, ideally, that both women and men will see every option with the same shade of *do-or-die* or *suck-it-and-see*.

So, are we prepared to accomplish Beauvoir's vision by removing women's soft options? Will we make these sorts of changes in the interests of equal opportunity in the workplace? If not, then we are stuck in a division of labor based on gender roles. This division of labor has nothing to do with patriarchal oppression, and everything to do with biology. If we want to establish true equality in the workplace, then the only way to do it is to change biology, thereby changing the cultural options that depend on it. And we do this by making the sterilization of girls a compulsory rite of passage that always gets done before they are able to reproduce, like their mothers before them and their grandmothers before them.

True, there are some minor glitches in this strategy that need to be ironed out, but at least it is more realistic than the current trashing of men's rights in the interests of an "equality" that never was; an "equality" that relies on denying men their rights, and disregarding the complex web of risks, demands and complexities that color men's options.

# CHAPTER 7

# ARE ALL WOMEN GOLD DIGGERS?

We all know the popular feminist mantra that has infiltrated into mainstream culture, and it goes something like this:

All men are rapists.

We can also play that game:

All women are gold diggers.

What further proof do we need than the simple observation that the industry most often associated with the selling of love for money, prostitution, is dominated overwhelmingly by women?

But, I digress. If the propaganda that all men are rapists continues to be encouraged and promulgated throughout society and through every form of media, then we have a duty to explain how all women, indeed, can be considered be gold diggers. Let's explore.

From JW Productions comes a movie with a deliberately provocative question in the title - *Are all men pedophiles?* (Breure, 2016)[1]. This seems like an odd title, given that they acknowledge in the film the existence of female pedophiles. But if they want to take advantage of some kind of dominant cultural narrative, well, we can play that game too; indeed, it might be quite fun.

*JW Productions* (2016)[2] provides a brief outline on their website:

> For the first time in history the tables have turned on men. In the past "Witch-Hunt" was associated with women but now it is associated with men.
>
> In an effort to protect our children society has started to isolate men. This documentary explores the pedophilia hysteria and how all men are viewed as potential pedophiles.
>
> How did society come to such a conclusion and what are the political and social consequences?

Witch-hunts serve little purpose in the course of reason, and focusing only on the perversions of men doesn't help anyone. The perversions of women also deserve scrutiny and, for balance, we ask… are all women gold-diggers?

## Materialism as women's porn

E.L. James' novel *Fifty Shades of Grey* might pique women's curiosity, and they might fantasize about having nasty things done to them by a mysterious, powerful, rich dude that flies helicopters and owns lots of stuff, but their fantasies cannot be disengaged from the stuff that lies at the center of women's being. It is no accident that the main protagonist in the novel, Christian Grey, is obscenely wealthy; that he is mysterious, powerful and eager to indulge is part of the context that revs women's engines, but these are not the first things that a woman will notice.

The key to understanding what makes women drool lies in their self-indulgence; their narcissism; the me, me, me of the female psyche. And a primary vector for their self-indulgence is their materialism; their obsession with owning stuff. In a nutshell, women identify with stuff, it is the source of their *raison d'être*. Women's indulgent materialism is the shallow extension of their *hypergamy* (Tomassi, 2016)[3].

Women love stuff. Lots of stuff. They crave for stuff, the more the better. Women fall over themselves in the rush to obtain stuff… stuff on sale, *stuff at bargain-basement prices* (Lunchboxcafe, 2013)[4].

Women will *stampede shopping centers* (Bailey, 2011)[5] in the rush to acquire stuff. Women have special days on which they can celebrate and worship stuff... Christmas sales, stock-clearance sales, new fashion sales, spring sales, summer sales, winter sales, autumn sales, because-you're-worth-it sales.

Women wallow in stuff, they celebrate men who provide them with stuff, and they divorce men quicker than they can say "alimony and child support", should they find someone who can provide them with even more stuff.

Stuff doesn't even have to be useful. An obscenely expensive diamond ring, about as useful as tits on a bull, will nonetheless have women oohing and ahhing, and swooning in either admiration or envy, depending on who it is that is wearing it.

A woman might know nothing of the precision engineering, the exquisite upholstery and amazing technology that's gone into the creation of a high-performance Lamborghini Diablo, and she might not even know how to drive. But as stuff in which to sit and show off her latest perm, with a rear-view mirror that she can look into to make sure she's looking her best, it can make the ideal birthday gift from the man who has everything.

Women judge each other according to the stuff they own... big, shiny, gleamy stuff that sparkles in the sun and that they proudly show off to friends. Women judge each other according to the stuff that they wear and the stuff that they lather on their faces to provide the *masks that spell identity* (kerry-washington.us, 2009)[6].

Imagine where women would be without stuff. Imagine them coping in a world without cosmetics, without texting or Facebook, without the internet to follow for the latest fashions, or without television to keep up with the latest celebrity gossip (incidentally, notice how all these things on which women depend are created by men? Just sayin').

Where most men are content with four pairs of stuff, one for summer, one for winter, one for formal and one for casual, women want hundreds of pairs of stuff - sometimes even thousands - to match their lipstick, their mood, their dress, the occasion, the weather, the car, the furniture. So let us take this moment to spare a thought for *Imelda Marcos after her tragic loss of thousands of pairs of stuff* (Oliver, 2012)[7] and what she must have been be going through.

# Designer stuff

*Unmasking Feminism* (2010)[8] nails what women want:

> She may have everything she wants, but not everything she needs. She wants independence, the vote, her own income, etc., but she wants all these things like she wants a designer purse.

Precisely. Women want careers and self-determination like they want designer purses, shoes 'n' stuff. Independence, the vote and an income are fun things to have that make you look good, they create a good impression, and your girlfriends will envy you. They have nothing to do with achievement, responsibility, what you stand for or what you believe in. That's men's stuff.

For women, the role of minister of defense is more a fashion statement than it is a responsibility. Consistent with Angela Merkel's stance on refugees, *the defense ministers of Norway, Sweden, Netherlands and Germany* (Oltermann, 2014)[9] care less for protecting their countries from invaders than they do for maintaining appearances – you know, the kinder, gentler, friendlier face of a liberal, progressive Europe that holds its doors open for anyone, regardless of how their cultural and religious values clash with those of their own people. Fashionable, trendy and popular, they'll show that boring, stodgy old-boy network of The Patriarchy how defense should really be conducted. Hennis-Plasschaert, defense minister of the Netherlands, told the Guardian:

> "[The Dutch politician] Neelie Kroes once said to me that old boys' networks are the oldest form of cartels we have in Europe. She was right, but things are changing, and women can do similar things now."

And the Guardian gets right into the swing of it:

> Her tweet with the photograph soon went viral. To many, the image heralded a new era in which even the last bastions of male privilege were no longer closed to talented women. Sweden's foreign minister, Carl Bildt, retweeted it with the comment "True Power Girls" (and was widely criticised for the condescending tone).

Thank god for affirmative action, whether as formal policy or implied in the cultural narrative, without which these women would have had to compete against men on a level playing field. Without affirmative action, whether formal or implied, there is every likelihood that they might have opted for the safer, less stressful stay-at-home option. *Minister of Defense* is the ultimate designer label that a woman can flash around to all her friends. And relaxed in her self-assured superiority of her sex, she need not trouble herself with the boring details of her culture unraveling.

## Visceral sense of unfairness punches you in the gut

Women cannot understand that for men, work is not a hobby. They don't understand that for men, work is not something you do if you like, something you do if your fancy takes you. And so, women have acquired a visceral sense of the deep unfairness that only men have been allowed to enjoy access to these goodies for centuries. It hits them in the gut like a pile-driver. Now, thanks to feminism, things are different. For women steeped in the culture of feminism, they can now enjoy work as an option, an indulgence, something they do if it's convenient and fun and does not interfere with their quality of life. That's why women need affirmative action, so that they can have first choice at those jobs selfishly and insensitively being hogged by men who have families to support.

A woman's perspective may be narcissistic and self-indulgent, but it has very practical survival benefits, and enables them to cope with the unfairness of thousands of millennia of oppression. Thanks to feminism, they now have more options. They can still prioritize being provided for and they continue to *judge men on their ability to provide* (Arndt B. , 2012)[10], classifying men as winners, losers, studs and creeps, as they have for millennia in the tradition of hypergamy. But now thanks to affirmative action, they are at liberty to toss their provider should they get bored with him. They can even claim child support and alimony if they want - and then take away another man's livelihood as payback for all those millennia of oppression against women. And if any man should get too uppity about his rights, she has VAWA to protect her "rights" (privileges) while trashing his *constitutional rights* (Wex Legal Dictionary)[11]. She can contrive *unsubstantiated allegations of rape or violence* (Kassam, 2016)[12] to put him back in his place; *and then expect to get away with it* (Franklin, 2014)[13]. Indeed these days, she can even *murder* (Davison & Hembling, 2014)[14] and the worst that she might expect is a stern look from the judge with a slap on the wrist.

## Practical implications

Women's hypergamy is inextricably entwined with their narcissistic materialism. While not all women are necessarily gold-diggers, the assumption that they all are is one that will stand a man in much better stead than any self-help theories, like PUA and Game.

We are reminded of Maslow's hierarchy of needs. Because women control sexual supply, they set different priorities. They choose materialism as their first priority because they can, and because their sexual needs will be met by default subsequent to their first priority being met.

For men, appearances can help, but not in the same way that lookin' good helps women. It especially helps if you look rich; if you look like you own the Lamborghini on which you are leaning, or the yacht on whose deck you are standing. Google the terms [gold digger prank] for some laughs. It is the size of a man's wallet, not his member, that makes all the difference. There is no mystery about women at all, this is the simple, unvarnished truth.

The *Hot Crazy Matrix - A Man's Guide to Women* (Yeager, 2019)[15] provides a humorous take on the different priorities that men and women place in pairing with the opposite sex:

Where Yeager's hot/crazy matrix for men describes how men prioritize their choices in women, his money/cute matrix for women describes how women prioritize their choices in men. For women, the hot-crazy matrix does not apply. Instead, women have a money/cute matrix bounded by a horizontal "money" axis along the bottom, and a vertical "cute" axis on the left. For women, a huge no-go zone dominates the lower-left quadrant, where they put men who are neither cute nor have lots of money. However, once a certain point is reached along the money axis, a vertical line extending upwards and downwards to infinity, in both directions, defines the bounds of the husband zone. To the right of this vertical line, within the husband zone, it is no longer relevant how hot a dude is. If he has sufficient money, he is husband material, case closed. As in prostitution, so too, in love, for women, money plays a fairly central role.

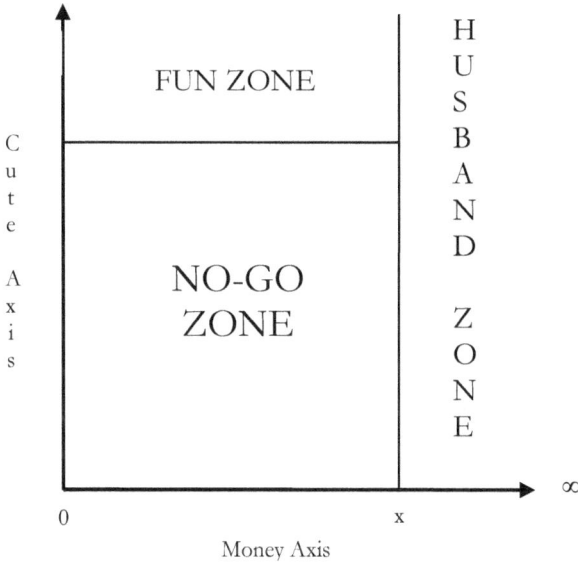

Money-cute matrix for women (Yeager, 2019)[16]

Notice, for the women's money-cute matrix, the absence of numbers on the axes. This is not a thoughtless omission on my part. Because all women are at least a level 4 crazy, things like mood, time of month or the weather can impact on how they rate their priorities. "Cute" is often volatile and unpredictable because it is hormone-dependent. What is cute today might be a creep tomorrow; what is creepy today might be a husband tomorrow. This is why learning Game can be effective for men. It taps into women's arbitrary whims that have them flipping one way on one day, or flopping another way a week later. Learn to press the right buttons, with Game, and much of the uncertainty can vanish.

James Yeager's Hot-Crazy and Money-Cute Matrices are all in good fun, but they are consistent with hypergamy theory and gender roles in the context of provider and provided-for. Money whispers to women in a way that it does not to men.

## It's a numbers game... for some

Of course, we can apply an analogous interpretation of Yeager's matrices to also make fun of PUAs. Just as an infinitely extending vertical line intersecting the horizontal money axis defines, for women, the lower limit of their husband zone, so too, an infinitely extending vertical line intersecting the hot axis defines, for PUAs, the minimum level of hotness that every PUA believes his birthright to never have to stoop below, regardless of how under endowed or broke he might be. This is just an expression of the biology of fertilization, with huge numbers of sperm hitting on a single egg. Only one sperm ever gets lucky.

And hence evolves an approach practiced among a significant segment of men... the so-called "numbers game." The most under endowed among PUAs often think nothing of hitting on the most out-of-their-league women. They think that they have nothing to lose. And, well, if they have no self-respect to begin with, then maybe they have a point. But they spoil it for other men, who must contend with the toxic miasma that swirls around women's narcissism. Women's narcissism does not come from genes. It does not come from within. It comes from without, from the inflated validation that women receive from men.

## The egg always has the last word

It is fascinating that what plays out socially between men and women, also plays out at the level of the gamete, between sperm and egg. Might this "gamete model of social engagement" that we first introduced in chapter 1, point to a fundamental principle in biology that the life sciences have thus far failed to articulate? Every sperm, healthy or degenerate, vibrant or sluggish, wants its piece of the action, and they will all work themselves into a frenzy to penetrate her resistance. But it is the egg that decides which sperm makes it through to her husband zone.

## Conclusion

Women certainly have primal sexual impulses that are no less than those of men, but these are typically sublimated in favor of materialistic priorities. This is why an appropriate response to the question "are all men pedophiles?" is, "are all women gold-diggers?" For the simple truth is, many of them are; and the assumption that *all* of them are, is the safest, most reliable assumption that a man can count on - more reliable than Game or anything that any woman or feminist might tell him. Everything comes together under this one assumption, the single insight that every woman is, at a primal, provided-for level, a gold-digger. All of women's choices, from the sublime to the ridiculous, are governed by it. The right assumption will predispose a man to the most astute of decisions, from the pleasures in which he indulges and the company he keeps, to defending his freedom and protecting his assets, to not wasting his time on spent women. Even the nicest, kindest, most marriageable women are not averse to being wooed by a man of means; how can a man lose by sticking with that one assumption to govern *all* women?

Are all men rapists? Are all women gold-diggers? Of course, both assertions are bigoted nonsense. But the former has been propagandized throughout mainstream culture and accepted, well, just what men are. The latter assertion is just as valid as the former, but it will nonetheless bring out the pitchfork-wielding mob demanding a lynching. Only we can play the same game and beat them at it.

Ultimately though, we can no more say that all women are gold-diggers than we can say that all men are rapists, for the simple truth is that women have as significant a role as men in the evolution of all that is good and bad in culture.

# CHAPTER 8

# SUCCESS OF FEMINISM, FAILURE OF SCIENCE

## Judge a culture by the company it keeps

Throughout the greater part of the past half century, from the sixties to the present, leading scientists often considered themselves allies to the feminist cause. Stereotypically, Steven Pinker and Richard Dawkins, as high priests of atheistic science, certainly considered themselves feminists. I don't know if they still do. They are intelligent men who, I am confident, would be open to changing their minds in the face of compelling evidence, were they to find sanctuary away from the overwhelming cultural miasma. But the mere fact that they did consider themselves feminists at all provides sufficient cause for concern regarding the science for which they've been among its most outspoken advocates.

Paul Zachary Myers is another biologist who continues to be staunchly feminist, at this time of writing. I have, on occasion, been impressed by his ability to see through the bs in determinism and scientism. And then he goes and spoils it all when he blocks anyone who dares criticize feminism. Unlike Pinker or Dawkins, he is less open to changing his mind in the face of compelling evidence, if it conflicts with his cherished feminist dogma. That sort of dogmatism does not a good scientist make.

That a movement as patently ridiculous as feminism should continue to align leading scientists in support, should cast serious doubt on the credibility of what science has become.

In his opening paragraph, Douglas Galbi (2015)[1] introduces Pinker's 2011 book:

> Harvard professor Steven Pinker is a superstar scholar and a champion of science and truth-seeking. His book, The Better Angels of our Nature: Why Violence has Declined, is an international best-seller. Mark Zuckerberg and Bill Gates, who each are probably more influential world-wide than any politician, lauded Pinker's book. Pinker's book explains that prior to the eighteenth century, or perhaps prior to the past few decades, women had no rights, men held women as property, and men could rape and beat women with impunity. But much more work remains for men to do to protect women...

Galbi then proceeds to make short work of thoroughly debunking the feminism that informs Pinker's gynocentric narrative. It is indeed disturbing that "superstar scholars, champions of science and truth-seeking," and the elites that look to them to inform their entrepreneurial and cultural visions, are representative of the symbiosis between a broken life-science paradigm and the cultural values that are informed by it.

Most of these elites are intelligent folk who are not paying attention to the craziness that is unraveling before their eyes. Their addiction to the groupthink, the fashion and its rewards overrides their ability to think critically, to pick it to pieces. Instead, they take to signaling their virtue like ducks to water, and truth is relevant only so long as it conforms to the accepted, politically correct narrative.

In the continuation of this resilient spirit of the elites, esteemed biologist, promulgator of selfish-gene theory and founder of memetic theory, Richard Dawkins himself embraced the feminist narrative and had taken to virtue-signaling his feminist-friendly credentials. For a while on internet blogs, I recall that he had taken to referring generically to the person volunteering as a subject in an experiment, with the personal pronoun "she" instead of the generic "he" that has been our tradition for centuries.

Dawkins has, on several occasions in tweets and blogs, proclaimed his support of feminism. He and Pinker are not the only ones. Their misguided willingness to associate with feminism raises concerns about critical thinking in contemporary science. If we take Pinker and Dawkins as representative of science as a whole, then science in general is seeking to align itself with a political ideology that doesn't understand the most basic fundamentals of logic or reason. Consider, for example, feminists' relentless parroting of the wage gap myth, with its reliance on the "77 cents in the dollar" mantra. To this day, given the persistence of this myth that refuses to die, feminists don't understand what the mathematical concept of "average" or "median" means. The mathematics of average and median are certainly not rocket science, and nowhere near as complicated as integral calculus. And this is the fundamentalist crowd with which Dawkins chose to align himself.

Given these unsettling trends in science towards the politically correct, there are grounds to be concerned that science has become unscientific.

The failure of our life sciences to nip feminism in the bud is symptomatic of the failure of all our sciences, for it confronts the most basic premise of the scientific method. Our "hard" sciences have become flabby. Science faculties coexist with women's studies faculties at universities throughout most of the western world, with graduates from women's studies faculties sporting the same titles as graduates from science faculties. You will find doctorates and PhDs also in women's studies faculties.

## The unraveling of science and culture

Writing for the New York Times, Carl Zimmer (2012)[2], with reference to the findings of Dr. Ferric C. Fang and Dr. Arturo Casadevall, discusses the sharp rise in retractions of articles written for scientific journals. These retractions were cited as "a symptom of a dysfunctional scientific climate." One explanation for this erosion of standards suggests that we follow the money. It relates to how research grants are awarded, and the politicization of agendas.

In The Lancet, Richard Horton (2015)[3] laments the breakdown of our peer-review process, writing, "much of the scientific literature, perhaps half, may simply be untrue... The apparent endemicity of bad research behaviour is alarming."

Mathias Binswanger (2013)[4] notes that beginning in the 1960s, in the spirit of extending the availability of tertiary education to the masses…

> … the government has given up its reservations towards universities and formerly proud bastions of independent thinking have turned into servants of governmental programs and initiatives. Lenin's doctrine applies once again: trust is good, control is better.

We can anticipate these trends in research grants, programs and initiatives to work out especially well for propaganda-friendly education in areas such as women's studies and critical race theory.

We should judge a culture by the company it keeps. The company that our science faculties are keeping does not bode well for our sciences. Nor our cultures, for the rot pervades throughout.

*Fake News*, as an extension of our broken science paradigm, now pervades throughout culture. When a culture loses touch with reality and lies are accepted as truth, we've entered into a new kind of Orwellian nightmare. Feminism and the Matriarchy that it betrays is only a small part of the absurdity that constitutes contemporary Clown Culture.

Quoting the late Andrew Breitbart, "politics is downstream from culture." Feminism began first as a cultural phenomenon. It is an extension of cultural narratives striving to repackage the identity of Woman. In their attempts to realize the feminist dream, the cultural was personal and the personal became political. The connection between culture and politics is inextricably linked. If politicians do not address the clown in culture, if they fail to understand the interplay between culture and politics, then politics itself will reflect the groupthink that governs culture. Hence the relevance of George Orwell's famous novel, 1984.

Orwell's "War is Peace, Freedom is Slavery, Ignorance is Strength" thesis is brought into line with the current state of affairs, with the addition of a few simple lines:

- Truth is hate speech;

- Looting is protest;
- Fascists are anti-fascists;
- Anti-male sexism (feminism) is equality;
- Those who object to feminism (anti-male sexism) are sexists.

The contortions required to accomplish these feats of cognitive dissonance outdo anything in Orwell's imagination. If you object to sexism (of the feminist kind), then you are a sexist (of the misogynist kind). Clearly, these narratives are not concerned with universal principles that apply to everyone, but with asserting one's own tribal truths above all others.

The influence of the feminist juggernaut extends into areas that never even thought of themselves as feminist. Conservatives these days bend over backwards to accommodate the feminist agenda, for fear of being called sexists. The Chancellor of Germany, Angela Merkel, may be famous for her reluctance to call herself a feminist, but the "refugee crisis" that she started in Europe in 2015 could never have come about without the politically correct, anti-patriarchal "racist" shaming that became entrenched in our cultures with feminism. The "refugees welcome" banners carried by European women were inspired by distinctly anti-patriarchal, feminist narratives. The absurdity of this feminist-friendly agenda reached unprecedented levels, in its support of religious backgrounds that have extensive histories of denying women basic human rights. Feminists are quick to chastise white men as misogynists and rapists, but turn a blind eye to migrants from Middle-East countries raping women, when it does not suit their narrative.

This is the feminism that has garnered the support not only of scientists and academics but also politicians and corporations.

# CHAPTER 9

# SPIRITUALITY, THE DOMAIN OF MEN

Pickup Artistry (PUA) has become an industry, and a topic that frequently comes up within PUA circles is the so-called "natural". He is a man who is so good with women that it's instinctive. He doesn't even need to think about it because, of course, he's natural. The natural has acquired an almost legendary, folklore status as a hero to which PUA hopefuls can aspire. But what, exactly, is a natural? What skills does it take to move effortlessly in social circles, acquiring a following of women behind you like a Lothario Pied Piper?

The PUA industry promulgates the idea that a man can acquire the indispensible skill set that will make him a natural with women. PUA Game, or PUA for short, defines this skill set. A strange beast indeed, is this natural. He aspires to be a dominant alpha, and yet he calibrates his dominance to women's approval. Cognitive dissonance much? He invests in learning the right skills. He learns about the importance of social proof (*ref* glossary), about the need to display his social status. He poses and preens, displaying his dominance; then peeks out from behind his fingers to see if they're noticing.

How could you be dominant if you need to calibrate your dominance to what others think of you? You might masquerade your dominance, and you can pretend all you want that you don't care, and that it's how the world works, and the world requires it of you. And it might even get you laid. But the mere act of calibrating your behavior to the expectations of others defeats any hope you might have of aspiring to something better. Yes, you might attain your intentioned objective. But no, you are no dominant. You are deluding yourself, because you are playing into a fake cultural narrative. Some PUA bottom-feeders might be good with that. Secure men who are seeking to live and measure themselves by their own standards are not. Many are looking for guidance, and at least subconsciously, they are aware that there is something inauthentic about the PUA masquerade. It is to them that this chapter reaches out.

PUAs fancy themselves as alphas with harems, much like Suleiman the Magnificent or Genghis Khan were alphas with harems. But PUAs are neither Magnificent nor Khan, and they are certainly not alpha.

It is not women's dumb choices that should set the standard for men's behavior, but men who should be laughing at women's dumb choices.

The calibration of one's conduct to the expectations of others relates to conformity within culture. Survival within culture demands conformity. But how far should one be obliged to take their conformity? To what extent are they permitted to express their individualism, bounded by the constraints of conformity?

## Culture versus individualism

Conformity is a matriarchal, female-centric priority. Conformity to cultural norms requires vigilance in how others interpret you. The man that learns PUA Game in order to impress women is rationalizing like a woman in order to be a man. He is relying on a female mindset in order to define his manhood, and that cannot end well.

Individualism, by contrast, values independence. Independence of conformity is independence of culture. There is only one way to truly acquire independence of culture, and this is where spirituality enters the conversation.

The male lion's swagger, the bull-elephant's majesty and the silverback gorilla's authority are attributable to the tests to which males of many species are subjected, within their ecosystems. Their individualism is forged under circumstances to which their female counterparts are not subjected.

By contrast, the male hyena's skulking body-language tells us that he negotiates compromises with his bullying matriarchs. His inauthentic, supplicating behavior provides him with momentary respite from being picked on. He is, throughout the course of his miserable life, denied access to higher levels in the pecking order that only the females of his clan are allowed to occupy.

There are other examples in the animal kingdom that have matriarchal social structures, such as the meerkat, but the spotted hyena provides insights that can be reframed within the context of the human experience. Regardless of whether we are talking about male feminists or PUAs, I would nominate the male spotted hyena as perhaps their most representative spirit-animal.

And, incidentally, female hyenas make pretty good feminists, too. Just as human feminists often try to emulate the worst of men in their behavior and appearance, so too, female hyenas, with their pseudo penises, their dominating predisposition to the male and their larger bodies, bully male hyenas into a permanent state of submission. Female hyenas allow only other female hyenas, to the exclusion of males, into the higher levels of their hierarchies. Not unlike feminists in HR departments, who promote females over males in the interests of "equality".

Actually, female spotted hyenas out-feminist the original (human) feminists. A hyena's pseudo-penis, which also doubles as a birth canal, needs to be retracted in order to reveal her vagina, before the male hyena can mate with her. Mating cannot happen without her full cooperation. This would be the answer to feminists' prayers, as a nature-endowed device that keeps out those pesky male rapists. How cool would that be?

# Western cultures have changed

The sexual revolution of the sixties, attributable in large part to the introduction of the contraceptive pill, ushered in unprecedented changes in culture, and the way that men and women relate to one another. By dramatically reducing the inconvenience of ill-timed pregnancy, the contraceptive pill has impacted on the cultural narrative in important ways. Contemporary feminism could never have occurred without it.

In contemporary culture, we face a deluge of pornographic images, online, on billboards, in newsagents. This relentless immersion continues to remind men of their "needs," rewiring the brains of men who become ever-more convinced of the "needs" that are said to be programmed into their DNA. And it continues to rewire the brains of women who come to believe that all men are rutting, drooling hound-dogs who are only ever after one thing. All this, ultimately, thanks to our contraceptive technologies. And as the rewiring proceeds, it is easy to forget that women also have within themselves the primal motivations that are in no way less than the primal motivations of men.

A line has been crossed. What was previously forbidden by culture becomes more than a cultural norm; it becomes edgy and progressive. Culture is a whole, and it adapts. The trickle becomes a flood, and groupthink, with its obsession with fads, idolatry and hedonism, becomes the new norm. With new cultural benchmarks, peer pressure replaces family values. Game becomes the province of shysters and conmen along with the needy and the desperate, while women's hypergamy tends increasingly towards the characteristics of prostitution in its opportunism, crassness and arbitrariness. As culture transforms to the new standard, its character changes, and opportunism based in self-interest would seem to be its most enduring feature.

As a commodity with both monetary and cultural value, sex as a leisure activity, kick-started during the sexual revolution, played a crucial role in the rise of feminism. The relationship between the success of feminism and the rise of our contraceptive technologies is not an accident. By commoditizing sex, feminism mobilized chivalry and prostitution in new ways. Feminism is both chivalry and prostitution, in that it depends on female sexuality to get its way.

Feminism is chivalry in that it is simply a restatement of our established tradition of pedestalizing women. And it is prostitution in that it relies on chivalry to extract freebies for women at the expense of men.

# The problem with PUA

PUAs think they're being edgy, alpha and red-pilled in their implementation of PUA to seduce women. But they're just playing into the very narrative that they mock. The sexual revolution upon which they rely for their validation began as a feminist revolution. They have feminists to thank for it.

What choices people make in the course of their lives, provided they do not impact adversely on the lives of others, is perhaps none of our business. But PUAs *do* impact on our lives, because they impact on the cultural narrative. They artificially inflate the value of women.

These days we often hear about women's narcissism, and how even the drabbest among women are narcissistic attention whores. Guess where they're getting it from? They're getting it from the sexualized culture which PUAs help create.

Women do not have a narcissism gene. The narcissists that they become might begin in the mirror. But upon graduating from Family as entitled princesses, narcissism is plied into them by the countless spermatozoa that vie for their attention, and this becomes their addiction that is impossible to treat.

### *Investing the effort – is it worth it?*

It takes enormous effort to bother with this PUA stuff. Many a woman is easy enough to bed, provided that you take her with confidence, like it's a foregone conclusion (this is the master key to good PUA Game). But most men with any self-respect can't do this. They experience a blockage because instinctively they intuit that it's disrespectful. Moreover, they can do without the ensuing drama. There is much to be reluctant about. And the moment that a man hesitates, she picks up on it, and spooks.

If that's not hurdle enough, there is also the illusion of women's beauty of which men could do well to deprogram themselves. In the absence of makeup and fashion, all women look rather ordinary. When a woman cuts her long hair to a cropped style, removes her makeup and puts on joggers and a track suit, she looks like a bloke. Ordinary. What the PUA has to fabricate, however, is that the made-up woman, with long, permed hair, manicured nails, sexy high-heels and provocative fashion, is somehow *intrinsically* sexy - her entire being is imbued with sexy-genes. Her scent drives rutting PUA hound-dogs crazy (protip: her scent is, actually, perfume that she buys at a store and applies herself towards the illusion that she wants to create; sexy is not in her genes). You'd have to be retarded to swallow this stuff. Either that, or you must force yourself to believe it, talk yourself into it and pretend that the illusion is reality.

And just as PUAs rely on success with women for their validation, so too, women must rely on cosmetics and sexualized fashion to pull it off. The fakes are inter-connected. Without her props, a woman is mostly invisible to PUAs. Cosmetics, fashion and accoutrements, adeptly employed, could make the difference between a 6 that's invisible and a 10 that's noticed.

Still not put off? What about the debasement of having to grovel for sex, while hiding behind an alpha veneer of sexual indifference? There is much cognitive dissonance to have to assimilate.

In his tweet of March 30, 2021, Chateau Heartiste:

> The best LTR prospects for women would be quasi-virginal men who have not had the beta beaten into them, or established players who are happy with their record of accomplishment and ready to slow down

Record of accomplishment? What accomplishment? The accomplishment of deluding yourself that this hamster-wheel charade is worth investing all your efforts into?

Coach Red Pill (2020)[1] suggests that the key to success with women is to treat them like nerds. I think he's onto something. It makes sense, after all – often timid and fearful, prioritizing security over adventure, women are the quintessential nerd. The rationalization hamster that characterizes women's over-thinking is a nerdy predisposition. When you think it through, considering the ease with which women are played by players, PUA Game is clearly

SPIRITUALITY, THE DOMAIN OF MEN

a strategy for manipulating the gullible. Gaslighting is a feature of PUA Game; negging* is, after all, a form of gaslighting.

On his tweet of April 1, Chateau Heartiste: "Game will do the same for any man; the successes with women build on each other until your alpha pose isn't a pose anymore" (no, it's not an April-fool's joke).

On April 2, he tweets: "Celibacy is living death."

Taking these two tweets together, it would seem self-evident that the conquest of women is vital to a PUA's self-esteem. To fail to receive that validation is "living death." The core principle behind PUA Game is, essentially, taking advantage of the gullible. Can you really consider yourself to be a true Alpha among men if your self-esteem revolves around having to take advantage of nerds?

Having said all this, I'm not sure that CH is the PUA he portrays himself to be. He understands women too well to be this shallow. I suspect he's trolling us, or maybe it's his way of changing the cultural narrative (if so, it's worked quite well, at least in the short term). As a means of tackling feminism, it would be a genius strategy. I've briefly thought of doing the same kind of thing myself; constructing a proxy for the purpose of delivering a message, planting a seed of cultural change. But, I digress.

The thing that makes women a challenge to bed is the exact same thing that makes them easy to bed. They are nerds. And when we factor in the gamete model of social engagement, they will choose only from among the spermatozoa that bother; that is, the types of men least likely to have a single spiritual bone in their body. If a man can't be bothered, he won't get the girl, regardless of how interesting he might be to women. As gullible nerds, women are too easily removed from the market, thus creating scarcity. It's no more complicated than that.

CH's tweet, March 31:

Badboys never talk about their work with their women. They always keep it fun, light, and teasing

Of course. Nerds need constant validation, they don't want to be bothered with serious, boring stuff. They need reassurance that you

---

* Negs are subtle put-downs expressed in a joking manner, to target self-esteem and to manipulate. *Ref* glossary

are fun, likeable and popular, and that you don't take yourself too seriously. Teasing is a fun way of demonstrating your dominance. Nerdiness is acceptable in women, not so in men.

Feminism itself is a product of female nerdiness. It takes a certain scale of gullibility to believe this nonsense. At what other point in history could such a ridiculous, cognitively dissonant movement have been taken seriously?

Neo-Darwinism again. Nerdiness is not in the genes. It's learned. The provided-for cannot be anything other than nerds... albeit, nerds with a huge responsibility. Motherhood.

Before our contraceptive technologies, biology regulated culture. But with the introduction of easily accessible hormonal contraceptives, we reengineered biology and it turned our cultures upside down. PUA is an artificial, unsustainable construct that owes its existence to feminism and the contraceptive pill.

## Slaves to illusion

If women are nerds, then what might that say about the PUAs who supplicate to women's manufacture of illusion (whilst pretending that they are not supplicating)? Let us take a closer look.

While I was at university, among the students in the dormitory where I was staying was a thin, geeky, plain-looking girl, a little taller than average, with cropped hair and coke-bottle glasses, to whom no-one paid any attention. Let's give her a name. Jane will do. As a serious post-graduate law student in her mid-twenties, Jane wasn't much fun, either. With a body language that was lanky and awkward, she would have scraped in a PUA rating of 4, maybe 5 at most (I'm being generous here; men who don't care to looker deeper than first impressions would probably give her a 2 or a 3, but most men are not this shallow or cruel). Either way, plain and invisible, that was Jane.

On one occasion, at a Halloween fancy-dress party, everyone rocked up in their colorful attire, from pirates, witches, warlocks and goblins to moguls, super-heroes, pimps and prostitutes. Jane was there, but no-one recognized her for quite some time. Without her coke-bottle glasses (she was wearing contacts) and her short, cropped hair concealed under her long, blonde wig, she was unrecognizable. There was something else about her that none of us had seen before. She was in high heels, wearing a sexy outfit with bare midriff. She had make-up on, skillfully applied, to transform her plain, featureless visage into a beauty with full lips, sexy eyelashes and clear, glowing skin. No longer lanky and awkward, her demeanor was graceful and elegant. She had come to our fancy-dress party as a prostitute; at least that was *her* glamorized idea of a prostitute. It became evident that this transformed beauty was attracting some serious male attention; and then it began to dawn on everyone that this was just plain, invisible Jane with coke-bottle glasses. "Wow, is that really Jane?" was the shared expression of astonishment that had changed the way that the males in our dorm would, from that occasion on, continue to see Jane.

Provided that a woman is fit and healthy and her proportions fall within normal limits, there is no reason why an average 5 cannot transform into a steaming 10... *provided that she knows, or is shown, the tricks of the trade*. A woman's body is the canvass on which she expresses herself. Men who understand how this works are ahead of the game, and they are best positioned to short-circuit the wiles of women.

Most men are rarely aware of the scale of the difference that packaging can make to a woman's looks. They might concede that perhaps a woman might improve her looks by 1 or 2, or maybe even 3 points at a maximum, along a 10-point scale. But men don't wear makeup or make provocative fashion statements, and so they never get to discover the before and after reactions that are contingent on packaging. How could they? They are not on the receiving end of all the attention.

Women, however, do notice. They say things like "people look at me differently when I wear my beautiful wig" (quoting here from a magazine article that I was glancing through in a doctor's waiting room). By people, of course, they mean men.

Men are inclined to the assumption that presentation is reality. When Plain Jane rocked up at our fancy dress party as a stunning blonde, they interpreted her transformation as her discovery of her untapped inner beauty, and they saw her differently from that day on. The extent to which a woman's presentation is manufactured illusion escapes most men. Women are also inclined to this assumption, but in different ways. "I wouldn't be seen dead without makeup" is a woman's expression of her belief that she needs makeup to be beautiful, without realizing that *all* women are trapped in their own manufacture of illusion. They believe their own bs, as it were.

Packaging and presentation make all the difference in the world. A tall, thin, dork with cropped hair wearing a tracksuit and joggers, ranking a PUA score of 4, can transform into a level-10 beauty with the skillful application of cosmetics, hair, scent and fashion. Body language also plays a big part. It helps to be proud and confident, instead of slumped and insecure. Presentation really is everything. It's the manufacture of illusion and women are experts at it.

And PUAs swallow it hook, line and sinker. If women are nerds, it follows that the men who allow themselves to be seduced by their manufacture of illusion cannot be too bright, either. Either that, or they are willfully ignorant. It does not pay to allow oneself to be swayed so easily in willful ignorance.

What might look like the hottest 10 in one context can look like the drabbest 5 in another. Whether it's actresses playing roles, like Charlize Theron in Monster, or actresses caught without makeup (google search terms – 'actresses without makeup'), it can be the difference between a fully hot tenner versus completely invisible fiver. It's all about culture and the illusions that constitute our cultural narratives. It's about manipulation of the cultural narrative, and understanding what buttons to push to make men take notice. The adeptness with which a woman is able to implement her beauty and fashion accoutrements makes all the difference in the world. Just as PUAs implement Game to push women's buttons, so too, women have their own techniques for pushing men's buttons, and it revolves around the manufacture of illusion.

Authentic spirituality is about overcoming culture's illusions. Supplicating to women's sexuality, regardless of how convincingly one might pull off their aloof alpha masquerade, is to remain a slave to the illusions that women manufacture. So long as these illusions provide the basis for a PUA's motivations, so long as his self-esteem is contingent on the validation he receives from successfully bagging women, then he cannot claim to be motivated by a spiritual agenda. He's failed to understand where his desires come from; how can he do otherwise? He's probably neo-Darwinian (despite never having undertaken formal studies in biology) and he thinks his motivations and his destiny are defined in his genes. Spirituality and PUA are diametrically opposed contradictions, and one is inviting serious cognitive dissonance to pretend otherwise.

Long story short, men can do themselves a big favor. You need never have another of those coyote moments (where you wake up and want to gnaw your arm off for fear of waking her). Just steer clear of PUA. It really is a mug's game.

## The real purpose of men

Ours is the first time in history that, for all intents and purposes, every man has access to sex. If he has problems engaging with women, he can pay for it, in the various forms that it is available, whether online or on the streets. It never used to be this way.

Throughout human history, however, many men have had to do without. Many failed to procreate, they failed to pass on their genes. For example, Diep (2017)[2], in interview with researchers Melissa Wilson Sayres and Toomas Kivisild, citing their team's work (Karmin, et al., 2015)[3], observes:

> Once upon a time, 4,000 to 8,000 years after humanity invented agriculture, something very strange happened to human reproduction. Across the globe, for every 17 women who were reproducing, passing on genes that are still around today—only one man did the same… "It wasn't like there was a mass death of males. They were there, so what were they doing?" asks Melissa Wilson Sayres… In more recent history, as a global average, about four or five women reproduced for every one man.

Other references in population genetics come to similar conclusions, for example, Baumeister (2010)[4] and Geggel (2014)[5]. Baumeister believes that the human population is descended from twice as many women as men; though in light of current research, this might err on the conservative. Favre & Sornette (2011)[6] churn through some calculations, and show that:

> Today's human population is descended from 10,000 to 100,000 as many women as men! In other words, for each male who made it today through his genes, 10'000 to 100'000 women made it!

This is interesting, but we have to be careful how we interpret it. Their conclusions are brought into a more moderate perspective, and confirm what the preceding references have, namely:

- Most ancient female ancestors have passed their genes to the present population.
- Most ancient male ancestors have not passed their genes to the present population.

So, what might all these different observations suggest about the role of men? If history and population genetics are our guide, then the priority of men is, as we've discussed previously, at the boundary between culture and the unknown beyond culture. The role of men is, essentially, a spiritual one.

Science and knowledge are, I argue, spiritual pursuits, and many of our greatest founders in science were spiritually or religiously inclined.

There are reasons why most of our sciences and world religions are inspired by men and led by men. Culture looks to women for its continuation, and to men for answers. Women are valued for what they are, and men are valued for what they become. Within western culture, it has traditionally been the role of men to lead, and that of women to follow. Now we can better understand why.

None of this is to suggest that women cannot do science. Far from it. There's some good, innovative work being done by women in the life sciences, for example. We have Dian Fossey to thank for some great research on gorillas and their social behavior; her work impressed me as the final nail in the coffin of determinism. I'd even suggest that women have played a major role in shunting us out of this neo-Darwinian cul-de-sac that we've been trapped in for far too long. But science is not the hill that women would choose to die on. For the majority of women, science is not their priority.

Insofar as women should be the spiritual soulmates of men, nobody wishes to exclude women from spiritual pursuits. What I want to emphasize is that the *priority* of men is a spiritual one, and it defines their primary purpose[*]. The moral imperative of good versus evil and truth versus lies is the responsibility, first, of men. Which

---

[*] Just as nobody wishes to exclude men from familial involvement, the *priority* of women is family, and it defines their primary purpose.

brings us back to the familiar bell curve, where geniuses and idiots occupy the tails of the distribution. The battle between good and evil is an expression of the same bell curve.

Our earlier insight bears repeating. The priority of women is security. The priority of men is liberty. Both come with their respective costs and benefits. The constraints of security limit women's freedom. The freedoms of liberty expose men to risk. This is why women have, throughout the millennia of human history, deferred to male leadership, and why they required men to bear the risks and responsibilities that leadership entails.

## Revisiting the three legs of the tripod

If spirituality is the domain of men, why then is procreation denied to most of them? Does it not make sense that those with the best genes (supposedly) do in fact pass on their legacy?

What is the average lifespan for humans? One hundred years as a ballpark will suffice, to make my point. What is a hundred years in the course of human history? Or in within the lifespan of our solar system, or galaxy? In the west, death by suicide for males is three to four times that of females. Why the rush? Life is so short, and there is so much to learn.

Many of us are born into families that are, to a greater or lesser extent, dysfunctional. The three legs of the tripod – mother, father and culture – provide us with three legs that define our lives. If one leg is broken, we have two others to provide us with direction. If two legs are broken, we have one leg to lean on. But if three legs are broken? What options do we have if, after surviving our dysfunctional families, our culture also turns out to be broken? Must we give in, and accept the terms of a broken cultural narrative? You can do that if you want. But for the very tiny one hundred years that constitutes the upper limits of the human lifespan, is it worth it? If a cultural narrative is ridiculous, why buy into it? It is far better and more rewarding to step beyond a ridiculous culture and a broken family, to discover new possibilities.

If the role of women is to pass on a genetic legacy, then the role of men is to pass on a cultural legacy. From science to religion, from philosophy to business, it is mostly men who have left their mark on culture. It's what men do. And it's what contemporary Clown

Culture is trying to erase. If this cannot stir men's ire, I don't know what can.

## PUA Game as spiritual death

Essential to the PUA agenda is the exact same thing that is essential to the feminist agenda. Neither is possible without our contraceptive technologies. The transformation of sex into entertainment is an artificial construct that is not sustainable. It requires massive transformations in culture and how people think.

Hormonal birth control tampers with biology in a way that is unnatural and unsustainable. It's not meant to be this way. In fact, with the sexual revolution, it has turned out to be a fascinating experiment. We've discovered that women's choices are not based in objective reason, but in impulsive, arbitrary encounters, and are contingent on the circles that they happen to stumble into. The happy (or not so happy) accidents of life's dumb chance. If they encounter pimps, they become prostitutes; if they encounter nerds, they become geeks; if they encounter losers, they become sluts; if they encounter thugs, they become damaged; if they encounter priests, they become virtuous; if they encounter wealthy magnates, they become kept women; if they encounter sugar daddies they become sugar babies. And so on. So much luck involved, but we don't see it because we assume that our genes are in the driver's seat, guiding our rational decisions.

From this fascinating experiment that is the contraceptive pill, we notice that women's choices are for the most part arbitrary, and therefore, often, incredibly stupid. For a man to emulate the men that women choose is, for the most part, in the contemporary zeitgeist, to emulate losers. Among the menagerie of losers that transition through many women's lives, there are very few heroes worth emulating. Before the contraceptive pill, there was hypergamy. Back then, the rules for men were simpler; just be good at what you do, be the best you can be, and you will be rewarded, honor intact. It was much easier being a success-object. With the mainstreaming of the contraceptive pill, however, hypergamy transformed into hyper-arbitrary; a world of labels, illusions and contortions where groupthink drives the narrative, and thugs and degenerates are conflated with dominant and exciting. The rational man must create his own alpha, and steer away from the paper alphas of women's dopey choices.

The manner in which culture has shifted would horrify our ancestors. Tampering with biology has serious consequences.

Many PUAs sense that there is a problem, but prefer to turn a blind eye to it, only too happy to compete for the spoils in their take-no-prisoners, existential war. Why should they care? Chateau Heartiste sees it, and acknowledges it. As has been noted earlier, he guesstimates that his aggregate sexual experiences would have amounted to about one tenth of his actual record, were it not for the ready availability of reliable contraception.

Some PUAs do recognize that there is a problem. Ex-PUA RooshV sees it, saw it was wrong, unpublished his books, became a Christian, and now devotes his time trying to undo what he had done.

## Where to from here?

Rollo Tomassi (2020)[7], with reference to his essay *Global Sexual Marketplace*, writes that today's globalization is not just about economics or demographics, but also applies to intersexual dynamics:

> Gone are the days when a young man or young woman could expect to meet one of the handful of eligible, single people in their high school, small town or limited social circle with whom to pair off and start a family with. In the *old order* young people were stuck with the choices of a limited, *Local* sexual marketplace. Today, with our instant, robust, forms of digital communication, a worldwide sexual marketplace has now opened up the romantic prospects of virtually anyone on planet earth with a smartphone and an internet connection. Don't like your prospects in your hometown? Now there's a whole world of men and women waiting to meet you. The *old order* of intersexual dynamics - and the old social contracts that the *Blue Pill* raised you to believe were still valid - has fundamentally shifted, and all in less than 20 years.
>
> The rapidity of this shift is what I believe is at the root of the problems that surround the new way of doing the *old order* institutions. As a global society we are still reluctant to let go of the, now apparent, falsehoods of those *old order* institutions; even

in light of the new order evidences and data collected as a result of this unprecedented access. While we attempt to reconcile our old beliefs with what a global information network confronts them with, we cling evermore tightly to what we thought we knew. This is a difficult transition because it formed the foundation of who we were in the prior order. And as we try to make sense of it we are presented with both true and false narratives that pander to the fact that this information and technology is progressing at a rate that most human minds were never evolved to keep pace with.

Tomassi raises important points that go some considerable way to explaining the predicament of contemporary, globalized homo sapiens. However, he presumes evolution theory in his book, as he makes clear in his introduction:

So let's get this out right here; I'm going to infer, refer to and presume evolution a lot in this book. *Evo-Psych* and *Evo-Bio* have always been principle frameworks for the *Red Pill* praxeology, and until something better comes along, that's what we have to work with.

As I've emphasized throughout this book, the neo-Darwinian paradigm makes assumptions about needs being determined in the DNA blueprint, and it is blind to the role of culture. As such it denies us agency, because it denies us the insight that it is the choices we make (from culture) that shape what we become.

Women don't have their beliefs about the world tested the way that men do. Women require what culture requires, because, like nerds, they accept culture's terms without questioning them. So, if culture tells *you* to do the Silly Dance, you do the Silly Dance. She is the ovum, relentlessly wooed by the countless spermatozoa who want to access her. If *you* refuse to perform, she will invariably stumble into a spermatozoon who does.

The power of women does not come from within. Theirs is not the power of personal agency. Their sexuality is not programmed within their genetic code. The power that women possess is the power that has been surrendered to them by men. Women crave attention from men, and they rely on validation from men. And they receive it in spades from the men that fawn over them; from the beta orbiters vying for their attention, to the PUA opportunists extracting sex from them. Like the male black-widow spider who submits to the larger female to be devoured by her, following his one-time opportunity at procreation, so too, the modern human male submits to the female in his relentless fawning over her and her unnaturally sexualized context. That's why even the drabbest among women often become narcissistic attention whores. We accept this situation as normal because we've accepted the deterministic neo-Darwinian narrative. "It's in our genes, we can't help it." But it's not normal. It's not in the genes. It is divergent with both historical experience and natural law.

Throughout most of human history, before contemporary feminism and the sexual revolution, men and women have paired up the old-fashioned way, through family, circles of friends and so on. Indeed, until about the 18th century, arranged marriages were the norm, worldwide. Were arranged marriages wrong? Is there a better way? Or is it we, with our gamete model of social engagement, informed by the neo-Darwinian narrative, propagandized in feminism and porn, and sustained by the contraceptive industry, who have it all so stupendously wrong? I don't want to be drawn into a conversation, at this point, on whether we should return to the ways of old. But one thing I will say is that the current situation will not sustain much longer. Our trajectory is third world and the destination is Dark Ages.

Tomassi is right about the factors that have brought to bear on the sexual dynamics of our time. But things are more complex than simply learning to accept the current situation. If it looks like a turd and stinks like a turd, then it's a turd. It would be counter to one's spiritual quest to embrace the turd. Perhaps, far from accepting the current situation, it will pay to recognize that a major existential crisis is looming on the horizon, for our cultures; we are under no obligation to step into it.

## Scientific spirituality

If science and spirituality are the domains of men, does this not present a contradiction? Isn't spirituality just subjective woo, while science is fact-based, smart and objective? How can one be both spiritual *and* scientific at the same time?

*This* is the central problem with the neo-Darwinian narrative. In its determinism, it fails to recognize the role of culture in wiring brains. There is no genetic blueprint in the DNA that determines how brains are wired. The wiring of brains is not bottom-up, but top-down. The *actual* direction of causation is, in effect, the reverse of that assumed in determinism. It is the choices that we make from culture that wire our brains. Insofar as personal agency is accompanied by the illusion that we have control over our destinies, it is the culture bearing down on us that has the greater impact on our predispositions, our habits, and ultimately, our lives and identities.

As we concluded in chapter one, we no longer have a mind-body problem. By integrating mind with body, we are better able to integrate human with culture. We are products of culture to an extent that we were unable to appreciate, back when we thought in terms of the deterministic paradigm with brains "directing" behavior.

And when we factor culture into our paradigm, we can better appreciate the role of individualism versus groupthink. Individualism is about lifting oneself out of the cultural miasma, and defining a path independently of the mob. It is about pushing the boundaries of the cultural known, and into the unknown, and becoming something that the culture is unfamiliar with. It is about transformation. It is about introducing a new narrative that the culture hasn't seen before.

We might call it individualism. Someone else might call it spirituality. Perhaps we need to invent a new term, to describe someone that thinks independently of the collective cultural hypnosis. There is definitely no woo in this spirituality of which I speak. What I have in mind is the most scientific life-science that there can be.

# CHAPTER 10

# CHOOSING YOUR RELIGION

Our trajectory in this book has taken us through the topic of spirituality, and this invariably brings us to the biggest of questions. Of all the world religions that are available to us, how should we decide on which one to follow? [Perhaps some readers believe that you can be *spiritual but not religious*. Bear with me; there's something here for you too].

Throughout this book, I've drawn attention to the problems with neo-Darwinism. The central problem is its deterministic, bottom-up direction of causation, based on the assumption that genes and the DNA blueprint account for not only biology, but also behavior. Neo-Darwinism is mostly blind to the top-down direction of causation. If genetic causation is bottom-up, then it is our engagement with the world that is top-down. Engagement with the world relates to culture.

Culture provides the templates for our identities, and the rules for behavior. And this is where religions are of significance. Religions are theoretical frameworks, as belief systems, providing the interface between personal identity and cultural identity. In the absence of some kind of belief system, as a body of shared assumptions, there can only be chaos. No culture can persist in the absence of a body of shared assumptions. Religions provide the means of making our shared assumptions consistent. If we doubt this, then one only need look at how contemporary America is splintering into different factions of belief that are inconsistent with one another.

If religion provides a vehicle for our spirituality, then how might we go about identifying a religion that best suits our needs? Each of us has our own priorities and therefore, our own criteria. My own priority is truth, and so my single criterion for deciding on which religion is fairly simple. I ask, which one is the most scientific?

Our contemporary cultures have access to insights and facts that our ancestors never had. For example, we know that the world is a sphere and is one of 7 other worlds that orbit our sun. We know about galaxies, and the unfathomably large number of them that exists, thanks to the Hubble telescope. We know that on average, each galaxy contains hundreds of billions of stars. We know about the amazingly complex structures of cells. We know about viruses and bacteria. What was it like among our ancestors, to drink stagnant, dirty water and never know why you got sick as a dog one day, or three days, or three weeks later? What was it like witnessing an eclipse, without knowing what a star, sun or moon actually was? Having to defer to one's sun and moon gods, Sol and Luna, or Helios and Selene, is something that is utterly alien to our modern way of thinking, given the facts that we now have at our disposal.

It kind of amazes me that despite all our knowing, we don't seem to have evolved all that far. It really does seem that the amount of stuff one knows bears little relationship to wisdom. I suspect that *not* knowing many things predisposes one to a humility that constrains the reflexive stupid that was so evident during Peak Clown of the 2020 US election.

## The things that we know

Before we review the merits of any of the religions, let us briefly summarize what we currently know; we can consider this our axiomatic framework:

- There is a difference between an axiomatic framework of principles that hang together in the pursuit of consistency, versus a cobbling together of arbitrary observations that do not prioritize consistency with one another. Isaac Newton's physics is a good example of the former. The life sciences are in dire need of the same kind of systematic, Newtonian thinking. Which religions can we regard as axiomatic frameworks that might aid us in the formulation of a more compelling life science?

- The principles of consciousness apply to all living entities. Motivation, association (associative conditioning) and habituation are fundamental to every organism, not just humans. This is the essence of a relatively new paradigm that is continuing to develop in the life sciences;

- The preceding point has implications for anthropocentrism, and the human exceptionalism that has plagued many religions. Humans are not "exceptional" and there is no such thing as instinct. The suggestion that we are has been the greatest stumbling-block to progress in the life sciences. The truth is that the principles of life that apply to cats and dogs, birds and fish, ants and bees, apply also to humans. My references to lions, elephants, gorillas and hyenas, in the preceding chapters, are not merely colorful metaphors, but expressions of this fundamental principle;

- Neural plasticity is integral to how the brain establishes its functional specializations. It is directly analogous to the "people plasticity" that enables a city to form into its functional specializations, such as industrial areas, residential zones, commercial hubs and business centers. Neural plasticity is essential to a proper understanding of the mind-body problem (Jarosek S. , 2013)[1]. I also make the case for DNA entanglement as a solution to the binding problem. This suggests an explanation for how the colony of neurons that constitutes the brain can bind into a unified whole, enabling the organism to act as an agent that makes choices (Jarosek S. , 2017)[2];

- From the preceding point, it follows that just as a personality is a thought, so too, a culture is a thought. One can take that as metaphorically or as literally as one likes, depending on the theoretical framework that they are assuming. For me, Peirce's "The man is the thought" (CP 5.314, in Peirce (1931-1966))[3] tends towards the literal;

- The neo-Darwinian paradigm has prejudiced our understanding of culture. That is, we assume that the only cultures that matter are those that have been recorded throughout human history, on Earth. In the spirit of anthropocentrism, these constitute our exemplars of "reality." The truth, however, is very much broader than that. The most advanced alien cultures, for example, are unlikely to be struggling with the merits of capitalism over communism, or determinism over religion. There are a great many cultural possibilities that exist, well beyond our capacity to comprehend them. The possibilities are as vast as the universe is big;

- Hubble Deep Field has revealed the universe to be big, very big, with uncountably many galaxies;

- The life-essential elements carbon, hydrogen, nitrogen, oxygen, phosphorus, sulphur (CHNOPS) that exist on earth have already been found on Mars in earlier rover expeditions. The atoms and molecules that are so essential to life on Earth are strewn in abundance throughout the cosmos. What exists over here, with all its predispositions and likelihoods, exists over there, stars and galaxies away;

- Entropy, as the tendency to disorder, must be taken seriously. The entropy relevant to living systems is that which relates to information theory (Claude Shannon). Neo-Darwinism does not properly address entropy. Whether a system is closed or open (thermodynamic, or Boltzmann entropy) is irrelevant to the degrees of freedom that relate to the tendency to disorder;

- The physics of our experienced world (what we call reality) are very different to the physics of the very small. There is no mystery about this. When you reduce the length/height of an entity, its mass (volume) is reduced by the third power. *Halving* the edges of a rectangular block of matter reduces its mass to one eighth. Extend that third-power reduction to the level of the atom, and the constraints of physics as we know them virtually disappear. Strange behaviors at the atomic and subatomic levels are inevitable. This is why such remarkable complexity is possible within cells and their DNA, why ants and spiders have long legs, and why the tiniest bugs appear like monsters from alien worlds, when viewed under an electron microscope. We can extend this third-power rule in the opposite direction; it is the reason why the bigger the animal, the stouter its form and the stubbier its limbs;

- To cut a long story short, our third-power reduction can obviate the need for a Creator. The void has within it the capacity to create all the complexity that is essential to life (as might be suggested in the fleeting appearance of virtual particles within the quantum void). Hence the relevance of quantum mechanics. No Creator required. Talking about the need for a Creator just passes the buck. It does not explain anything. Who created the Creator? A Creator-Creator, of course? By deferring to a Creator, we become willfully ignorant of a more interesting and plausible possibility, relating to the nature of the void and the physics that must spring from it;

- I am not saying there is no god. I am saying that the question is irrelevant to good science;

- Whilst no Creator is required to create "something", this is not to say that a unified consciousness won't emerge as perhaps a guiding influence. The possibility of a unified, collective intelligence is not unreasonable. This relates to nonlocality-theory in quantum mechanics. Some people might, if they want, call that unified consciousness God. If we are going to pursue a scientific trajectory, however, this is not something that we should allow ourselves to get bogged down in;

- The introduction of nonlocality into the narrative introduces the idea of the nonlocal self, and this invites interpretations that challenge our assumptions about the nature of self. These might be central to a more realistic life-science paradigm. There are far-reaching implications, particularly with regards to the determinism that has assumed the self to be an independent agent that answers only to its own survival.

Despite this list of conjectures, we do not yet have the foundation for a compelling life science. There is much that needs to be verified and substantiated. Such a list is necessary, nonetheless, in order to provide a review of the sorts of assumptions that we should be making when considering a life-science paradigm. It shows that we're paying attention.

Under this list of criteria, how might the different religions stack up? A detailed comparison of the different world religions is beyond the purpose of this book. However, I will briefly summarize why I choose a synthesis of Buddhism with Christianity, with the semiotic paradigm providing the theoretical framework to support it.

## Towards a scientific religion

Buddhism has much in common with Hinduism, given that it began as an offshoot of Hinduism. Hinduism is impressive in many ways, with its deeply moving scripture, and its insights obtained despite the absence of technology. However, unlike Hindus, Buddhists do not acknowledge a god or deity, and they do not believe in souls. Buddhists prefer the candle metaphor to describe reincarnation. That is, a soul does not migrate from one body to another, like it does in Hinduism. Instead, a self is reborn in the same way that a flame is reborn when a lit candle passes its flame onto another candle. Buddhism thus provides an interpretation of reincarnation that resonates with nonlocality in Quantum Mechanics, and extends it to the idea of the nonlocal self. As an axiomatic framework for a life science, Buddhism does an impressive job, given the technological limitations of the era of its founding.

The human exceptionalism of the Judeo-Christian and Islamic religions, however, precludes them from ever arriving at any compelling axiomatic framework for the life sciences. The notion of Man made in God's image is in desperate need of a Copernican-style revolution. The self-indulgent notion of Man at the center of all God's creation has no place in any religion that seeks consistency with good science.

The notion of Jesus as the Son of God is problematic. The notion of Jesus as one of the world's great prophets, however, has merit and can be taken more seriously.

Where Christianity fails in its human exceptionalism and its all-consuming reliance on a Creator, it succeeds in its reverence for truth and the greater good. The European Renaissance could never have happened without it. In valuing courage and standing up for what one believes in, Christianity provides the ideal antidote to groupthink. Buddhism's antidote to groupthink, by contrast, is more limited, given its inclination to defer to authority (e.g., filial piety). What is the distinction between groupthink and healthy culture? One clue lies in the *moral individualism* of Christianity, its relationship to courage, with Jesus as a role model. Groupthink is a feature of fear and cowardice, and it sticks like glue, turning people into unquestioning NPC-bots yearning for social approval and the need to belong. This is particularly evident in today's culture of social media. Hedonism and "fun" cultures are obsessed with needs and, despite their apparent freedoms and indulgences, are contained within strictly self-enforced limits revolving around social approval and popularity. How can you be free if you rely on the opinions of others for your validation?

Thus I arrive at my own solution for a religion to follow. It is a synthesis of Buddhism with Christianity. Where Buddhism tends to axiomatic consistency and reason, it does not connect with the greater good as Christianity does. Buddhism's filial piety, while a form of greater good, is also a form of exceptionalism that is not unlike the exceptionalism in Judaism.

There is no God as Creator. There is a greater good and there is a unity, preceded by the void. The void is predisposed to creation[*] and requires no Creator. A synthesis of Buddhism with Christianity resolves their contradictory narratives, and what one lacks, the other makes up for. This is a synthesis that works for me.

---

[*] For example, virtual particles of the quantum void.

# CHAPTER 11

# EPILOGUE

## Criticism of feminism is not criticism of women

As we approach the conclusion of this wide-ranging and interdisciplinary, albeit short, book, it is necessary to bring what we are trying to accomplish back into focus, This book is a critique of feminism and the broken neo-Darwinian paradigm that whispers its unspoken assumptions into their ideology. Neo-Darwinism is a problem because it provides the vaguely outlined forms against which feminists shadow-box. And in the course of making my point, I've shown that women can be just as capable of evil as men; that women are just as capable as men of abusing others. We need to be concerned how feminism, in its success in dismantling the matriarchal role to which women have aspired across the centuries, hurts not just men, but also women and children, in deeply profound ways.

This is not a Men's Rights Activist book. I've fought my own battles without looking to MRAs for support. This is not to say that men do not need support. Far from it. But my greater concern is the extensive harm that has been done to women and men in the name of feminism, and the scientism that provides the shadows in which feminists imagine their monsters to lurk.

# Taking stock of our competing paradigms

If it was not clear, within the first few pages, why the neo-Darwinian paradigm is of little utility in understanding women, men and their gender roles in culture, then it should have become more apparent by now. In accordance with the axiomatic framework introduced at the beginning of this book, if gender roles are habits, if gender roles are chosen, and if men and women like the gender roles to which they have been assigned, then it follows that:

- Women like nurturing and raising their children, they like networking with friends and family, they value security and being provided for, and they are drawn to the formidable in Man;
- Men like creating, discovery and adventure, they like competition, innovation and taking risks, they feel valued providing for their families, and they are drawn to the nurturing in Woman;
- Gender roles are complementary. Men's and women's different priorities establish the consistent narratives around which they structure their lives. That is to say, their different priorities relate to different responsibilities and different categories of choices;

By contrast, the neo-Darwinian narrative, with its emphasis on adaptive traits, sheds no light on the meanings that are integral to the complementary gender roles in culture. Within their narrative of sexual selection, for example, women choose successful providers and men choose fertile breeders because these are adaptive traits that propagate their genes into future generations. To be honest, what does that even mean? Neo-Darwinism provides little account of the meanings, motivations and experiences that explain men's and women's different, complementary choices in culture.

# Feminism trashes women's rights

Feminists claim to stand for women's rights, but they disempower the authentic center of women's matriarchal authority. They deny the role of women in everything that is good and bad in culture. They deny the role of the primary nurturer:

- Children first learn violence from their primary nurturer;
- Children first learn sexism from their primary nurturer;
- Children first learn from their primary nurturer who is expected to be the primary provider, and who is expected to be the primary nurturer;
- Most children eventually go on to become the adult men and women who continue the fine traditions that they first learned from their primary nurturer.

Feminism has done more damage to women and matriarchal authority than any other force in history. Feminism is not about observations of reality as it is, but projections of reality as feminists interpret it.

Feminism is a product of groupthink. It is an expression of the lumbering, heaving miasma of stoopid that is contemporary Clown Culture. Their toxic narrative revolves around virtue-signaling and shaming. Feminists rely on shaming in order to achieve their objectives. Shaming is the strategy you have when you don't have a strategy, and fundamental to its effectiveness is hate. If you're not too sure what to make of a feminist-inspired initiative, ask yourself if there is a shaming opportunity in it, a way of saying "look at how good I am, and how wicked you must be." This is manipulation and relational aggression at work. Shaming by feminists is pure projection. It makes sense. After all, feminism is a hate movement.

# Projections of a hate movement

The worst sexists in history have been those who invented sexism and its language, bringing its ugly face into high profile - the modern feminists. Even the original authentic feminists who began with legitimate concerns were sexists the moment that they overlooked the other equal half of the equation - women's complicity. In this, they have sown the seeds of feminism's own destruction.

What is complicity? The gender that is provided for says to the gender that provides, "I like what you do, do it some more." Irrespective of whether that more is war or commerce or invasion or ethnic cleansing or battery farming of animals.

Complicity is nurturing your little boys to be providers and your little girls to be provided for. Sexism is despising your provider while you cash the check that draws on their account.

And what is tyranny? The gender that is provided for says to the gender that provides, "your role is to provide, it is the ring through your nose; your identity, everything you are worth is in your duty to provide. Your mother first raised you to provide, and your father told you to man up and provide. We've been dependent on you for millennia and it's your fault, so now it's our turn. We want to be set free of you, we want the freedom to work if we want, or to stay at home if our fancy takes us. How good a provider are you? Are you financially secure? Can you keep us at home if that's what we choose? Why should we marry you when we can now provide for ourselves?"

Tyranny is getting the state to do your violence on your behalf. And the gender that is provided for demands of the men running the State that affirmative action be implemented so that the provided-fors have first access to the jobs that define the providers. If that's not Tyranny, then what is?

The worst sexists in history are the ones who accuse their opposite sex of being sexist, all the while denying the sexism that oozes from their very pores. The worst sexists in history are those who invented the word. They are our feminists.

# BIBLIOGRAPHY

Administration for Children & Families. (2002, December 31). *Child Maltreatment 2002*. Retrieved January 25, 2013, from Children's Bureau: http://archive.acf.hhs.gov/programs/cb/pubs/cm02/cm02.pdf

Administration for Children & Families. (2012, December 12). *Child Maltreatment 2011*. Retrieved January 25, 2013, from Children's Bureau: http://www.acf.hhs.gov/programs/cb/resource/child-maltreatment-2011

Allen, C. (2003, May 3). *Independent Women's Forum: We Love Guys: Return of the Guy*. Retrieved April 17, 2006, from Independent Women's Forum: http://www.iwf.org/articles/article_detail.asp?ArticleID=226

Amnesty International. (n.d.). *Female genital mutilation*. Retrieved April 17, 2006, from http://www.amnesty.org/ailib/intcam/femgen/fgm1.htm

Angelucci, M., & Sacks, G. (2004, September 15). *glennjsacks.com*. Retrieved from Research Shows False Accusations of Rape Common: http://www.glennjsacks.com/research_shows_false.htm

Anomalistic Psychology Research Unit (APRU). (2009, January 20). *Morphic Resonance, Collective Memory and the Habits of Nature*. Retrieved January 3, 2013, from APRU on Vimeo: http://vimeo.com/11653660

Archer, J. (2000). Sex Differences in Aggression Between Heterosexual Partners: A Meta-Analytic Review. *Psychological Bulletin, 136*(5), 651-680.

Arndt, B. (1998, October 10). Marginal Men. *Sydney Morning Herald*.

Arndt, B. (2012, April 22). *Why women lose the dating game*. Retrieved May 16, 2016, from The Sydney Morning Herald: http://www.smh.com.au/lifestyle/life/why-women-lose-the-dating-game-20120421-1xdn0.html

Australian Institute of Health and Welfare. (2000). *Media Release: Male Suicides More Common than Road Deaths*. Retrieved April 17, 2006, from Australian Institute of Health and Welfare (AIHW): http://www.aihw.gov.au/mediacentre/2000/mr20000711.html

Bailey, J. (2011, November 25). *Black Friday crowd rushing into Urban Outfitters*. Retrieved May 15, 2016, from [YouTube]: http://youtu.be/DigiWS1YhxI

Baskerville, S. (1999, December 22). Why is daddy in jail? *The Women's Quarterly, no. 18, Winter, 1999*(18). Retrieved January 24, 2013, from

http://www.stephenbaskerville.net/default/assets/File/Why_Is_
Daddy_In_Jail_1999_Wmn_Qrtly(1).pdf

Baumeister, R. (2010). *Is there anything good about men?: How cultures flourish by exploiting men.* Oxford University Press.

Beckett, F. (2008, November 11). *First world war: The men who would not fight.* Retrieved February 8, 2021, from The Guardian: https://www.theguardian.com/world/2008/nov/11/first-world-war-white-feather-cowardice

Belkin, L. (2003, October 26). *New York Times: The Opt-Out Revolution.* Retrieved April 17, 2006, from New York Times: http://www.nytimes.com/2003/10/26/magazine/26WOMEN.html

Bindel, J. (2012, November 29). *In love with a death row dandy.* Retrieved December 6, 2012, from New Statesman: http://www.newstatesman.com/lifestyle/lifestyle/2012/11/love-death-row-dandy

Binswanger, M. (2013, December 17). *Excellence by nonsense: The competition for publications in modern science.* Retrieved July 18, 2015, from Springer Link: http://link.springer.com/chapter/10.1007/978-3-319-00026-8_3/fulltext.html

Bjorqvist, K. (1994). Sex Differences in Physical, Verbal and Indirect Aggression: A Review of Recent Research. *Sex Roles: A Journal of Research, 30*, 177-188.

Breure, J. (2016, February 25). *Are all men pedophiles? Documentary.* Retrieved May 15, 2016, from [YouTube - JW Productions]: https://youtu.be/GeiIBZkDy4o

Buchanan, M. (2013, December 12). *Stephen Kamotho: A letter from Kenya.* Retrieved January 17, 2014, from A Voice for Men: http://www.avoiceformen.com/misandry/stephen-kamotho-a-letter-from-kenya/

Burrage, H. (2013, August 28). *Fighting Female Genital Mutilation With Our Keyboards: The Feminist Statement on FGM Is Launched Today.* Retrieved January 17, 2014, from Huffington Post: http://www.huffingtonpost.co.uk/hilary-burrage/fighting-female-genital-mutilation_b_3822317.html

Canetti, E. (1973). *Crowds and Power.* Penguin Books.

Carlton, R. (2001, August 19). *Human Bombs.* Retrieved January 25, 2013, from 60 Minutes: http://sixtyminutes.ninemsn.com.au/article/258824/human-bombs

Castleman, M. (2010, January 14). *Women's Rape Fantasies: How Common? What Do They Mean?* Retrieved January 19, 2013, from Psychology Today: http://www.psychologytoday.com/blog/all-about-sex/201001/womens-rape-fantasies-how-common-what-do-they-mean

cbresearch. (2007, November 7). *The Baby Brain Box / Dr. Jill Stamm Interview*. Retrieved December 30, 2012, from Youtube: http://www.youtube.com/watch?v=baek--_1ZfU

Chateau Heartiste. (2012, June 15). *More scientific evidence that chicks dig jerks*. Retrieved January 7, 2013, from Chateau Heartiste: http://heartiste.wordpress.com/2012/06/15/more-scientific-evidence-that-chicks-dig-jerks/

Chateau Heartiste. (2012, December 2). *Pope Paul VI On Birth Control Externalities*. Retrieved December 6, 2012, from Chateau Heartiste: http://heartiste.wordpress.com/2012/12/02/pope-paul-vi-on-birth-control-externalities/

Cherry, K. (n.d.). *Brain Plasticity: How Experience Changes the Brain*. Retrieved July 18, 2015, from About.com: http://psychology.about.com/od/biopsychology/f/brain-plasticity.htm

Cherry, K. (n.d.). *What Is Brain Plasticity?* Retrieved August 7, 2012, from About.com - Psychology: http://psychology.about.com/od/biopsychology/f/brain-plasticity.htm

Chesler, P. (2001). *Woman's inhumanity to woman*. New York: Thunder's Mouth Press/Nation Books.

Chesler, P. (2009). *Woman's Inhumanity to Woman*. Lawrence Hill Books. Retrieved January 17, 2014, from http://www.phyllis-chesler.com/books/womans-inhumanity-to-woman

Coach Red Pill. (2020, August 11). *Treat a woman like a nerd*. Retrieved March 7, 2021, from Coach Red Pill [YouTube]: https://youtu.be/EGKpS1wVqL8

Connolly, K. (2009, March 18). Fritzl's troubled childhood analysed in court. *The Guardian*. Retrieved August 7, 2012, from http://www.guardian.co.uk/world/2009/mar/18/psychiatrist-analyses-josef-fritzl

Crick, N. R. (1995). Relational Aggression: The Role of Intent Attributions, Feelings of Distress, and Provocation Type. *Development and Psychopathology, 7*, 313-322.

Crick, N. R., & Grotpeter, J. K. (1995). Relational Aggression, Gender, and Social-Psychological Adjustment. *Child Development, 66*, 710-722.

Davison, D., & Hembling, J. (2014, January 18). *Canada: A first world country*. Retrieved May 15, 2016, from A Voice for Men: http://www.avoiceformen.com/gynarchy/canada-a-first-world-cuntry/

Diehm, J. (2013, December 10). *1 In 9 Girls Marries Before Age 15, And Here's What Happens To Them*. Retrieved December 10, 2013, from Huffington Post:

http://www.huffingtonpost.com/2013/12/05/child-marriage-_n_4393254.html

Diep, F. (2017, June 14). *8,000 years ago, 17 women reproduced for every one man.* Retrieved 1 31, 2021, from Pacific Standard: https://psmag.com/environment/17-to-1-reproductive-success

Doidge, N. (2008). *The Brain that Changes Itself* (2008 ed.). Melbourne: Scribe Publications. Retrieved 12 6, 2012, from http://www.normandoidge.com/normandoidge.com/MAIN.html

Elam, P. (2011, March 26). *Mary kellett: This time it's for real.* Retrieved February 8, 2021, from A Voice For Men: https://avoiceformen.com/government-tyranny/mary-kellett-this-time-its-for-real/

Factory. (2011, January 15). *Answering a schoolgirl's questions.* Retrieved January 8, 2013, from A voice for men: http://www.avoiceformen.com/feminism/answering-a-schoolgirls-questions/

*Facts on Fatherless Kids.* (n.d.). Retrieved August 7, 2012, from http://www.photius.com/feminocracy/facts_on_fatherless_kids.html

Favre, M., & Sornette, D. (2011). *Cooperation-male-female_Boston28June11.* Retrieved January 31, 2021, from ETH Zürich: https://ethz.ch/content/dam/ethz/special-interest/mtec/chair-of-entrepreneurial-risks-dam/documents/Presentations/Cooperation_male_female_Boston28June11.pdf

FGC Education and Networking Project. (2003). *Facing Mt. Kenya - Jomo Kenyatta.* Retrieved April 17, 2006, from FGC Education and Networking Project: http://www.fgmnetwork.org/articles/kenyatta/index.html

Fiebert, M. S. (2005). *References Examining Assaults by Women on Their Spouses or Male Partners: an Annotated Bibliography.* Retrieved April 17, 2006, from http://www.csulb.edu/~mfiebert/assault.htm

Franklin, R. (2014, January 21). *Sara Ylen false rape claim shows ease with which innocent men convicted.* Retrieved May 15, 2016, from A Voice for Men: http://www.avoiceformen.com/feminism/feminist-governance-feminism/sara-ylen-false-rape-claim-shows-ease-with-which-innocent-men-convicted/

Friedan, B. (1976). *It Changed My Life: Writings on the Women's Movement.* New York: Random House.

Froomkin, D. (1998, October 1). *Washington Post: Affirmative Action Under Attack.* Retrieved April 17, 2006, from Washington Post: http://www.washingtonpost.com/wp-srv/politics/special/affirm/affirm.htm

Furchtgott-Roth, D., & Stolba, C. (1999). *Women's Figures: An Illustrated Guide to the Economic Progress of Women in America.* American Enterprise Institute. American Enterprise Institute.

Galbi, D. (2015, September 11). *Steven Pinker: sex, violence, and failure of enlightenment.* Retrieved September 16, 2015, from A Voice for Men: http://www.avoiceformen.com/gynocentrism/steven-pinker-sex-violence-and-failure-of-enlightenment/

Geggel, L. (2014, September 24). *Humanity has more mothers than fathers, DNA reveals.* Retrieved January 31, 2021, from LiveScience.com: https://www.livescience.com/47976-more-mothers-in-human-history.html

Gendercide Watch. (2012, January 31). *Case Study: Female Infanticide.* (A. Jones, Editor) Retrieved March 1, 2003, from Gendercide Watch: http://www.gendercide.org/case_infanticide.html

Gendercide Watch. (2012, January 31). *Case Study: The European Witch-Hunts.* (A. Jones, Editor) Retrieved March 1, 2003, from Gendercide Watch: http://www.gendercide.org/case_witchhunts.html

Gendercide Watch. (2012, January 31). *Gendercide Watch.* (A. Jones, Editor) Retrieved March 1, 2003, from Gendercide Watch: http://www.gendercide.org/

Glick, P., & Fiske, S. T. (1996). The Ambivalent Sexism Inventory: Differentiating Hostile and Benevolent Sexism. *Journal of Personality and Social Psychology, 70*(3), 491-512.

Glick, P., & Fiske, S. T. (1997). Hostile and Benevolent Sexism: Measuring Ambivalent Sexist Attitudes Toward Women. *Psychology of Women Quarterly, 21*, 119-35.

Graham, J. E., Marians, K. J., & Kowalczykowski, S. C. (2017, June 15). Independent and Stochastic Action of DNA Polymerases in the Replisome. *Cell, 169*(7), 1201-1213. doi: https://doi.org/10.1016/j.cell.2017.05.041

Green, C. D. (2007, September 13). *The Principles of Psychology, William James (1890)- Chapter IV, Habit.* (York University, Toronto) Retrieved January 3, 2013, from Classics in the History of Psychology: http://psychclassics.yorku.ca/James/Principles/prin4.htm

Gullace, F. N. (2014, June 30). *The 'White Feather Girls': Women's militarism in the UK.* Retrieved February 8, 2021, from openDemocracy: https://www.opendemocracy.net/en/5050/white-feather-girls-womens-militarism-in-uk/

Haier, R. J., Jung, R. E., Yeo, R. A., Head, K., & Alkired, M. T. (2005). The neuroanatomy of general intelligence: sex matters. NeuroImage, 25, 320-327. *NeuroImage, 25*, 320-327.

Harford, T. (2006, February 18). *I Do, I Do, I Do, I Do - The economic case for polygamy.* Retrieved January 20, 2014, from Slate.com: http://www.slate.com/articles/arts/the_undercover_economist/2006/02/i_do_i_do_i_do_i_do.html

Harrington, A. (2012, April 7). The fall of the schizophrenogenic mother –. *The Lancet, 379*(9823), 1292-1293. Retrieved August 7, 2012, from http://www.thelancet.com/journals/lancet/article/PIIS0140-6736(12)60546-7/fulltext

Hoogland, S., & Pieterse, R. (2000, November 1). *Wesley Mission: Suicide in Australia - A Dying Shame.* Retrieved April 17, 2006, from Wesley Mission, Sydney, Australia: http://www.wesleymission.org.au/publications/r&d/suicide.htm

Horton, R. (2015, April 11). *Offline: What is medicine's 5 sigma?* Retrieved April 4, 2016, from The Lancet, 385 (9976), 1380: http://www.thelancet.com/pdfs/journals/lancet/PIIS0140-6736(15)60696-1.pdf

Hutson, M. (2008, May 28). *Why Do Women Have Erotic Rape Fantasies?* Retrieved August 8, 2012, from Psychology Today: http://www.psychologytoday.com/blog/psyched/200805/why-do-women-have-erotic-rape-fantasies

Isenberg, S. (2000). *Women Who Love Men Who Kill* (2000 ed.). iUniverse.

Jarosek, S. (2013). Pragmatism, neural plasticity and mind-body unity. *Biosemiotics, 6*(2), 205-230. Retrieved from http://link.springer.com/article/10.1007%2Fs12304-012-9145-5

Jarosek, S. (2017). Quantum semiotics. (B. Goertzel, Ed.) *Journal of Nonlocality: Special Issue on Psi and Nonlocal Mind, 5*(1). Retrieved from http://journals.sfu.ca/jnonlocality/index.php/jnonlocality/article/view/64

John the Other. (2012, April 1). *Violence by proxy.* Retrieved January 20, 2013, from A Voice for Men: http://www.avoiceformen.com/feminism/government-tyranny/violence-by-proxy/

JW Productions. (2016). Retrieved May 15, 2016, from Are all men pedophiles? Documentary: http://areallmenpedophiles.com/

Karmin, M., Saag, L., Vicente, M., Wilson Sayres, M. A., Järve, M., & Talas, U. G. (2015). A recent bottleneck of Y chromosome diversity coincides with a global change in culture. *Genome Research, 25*(4), 459-466.

Kassam, A. (2016, March 26). *Canada urged to rethink approach to sexual assault after Ghomeshi acquittal.* Retrieved May 15, 2016, from The Guardian: http://www.theguardian.com/world/2016/mar/26/canada-justice-system-ghomeshi-acquittal-sexual-assault-allegations-approach?utm_source=esp

Kenyatta, J. (1965). *Facing Mt. Kenya* (1965 ed.). New York: Vintage Books. Retrieved from
http://www.fgmnetwork.org/articles/kenyatta/index.html

kerry-washington.us. (2009, April 18). *L'Oreal - 'Because you're worth it'*. Retrieved May 15, 2016, from [YouTube]: http://youtu.be/84SUfl8Yv4k

Kshatriya, R. (2012, October 3). *The ineffable mystery of Anglo hypergamy*. Retrieved January 7, 2013, from Anglobitch: http://kshatriya-anglobitch.blogspot.com.au/2012/10/the-ineffable-mystery-of-anglo-hypergamy.html

Kunkle, F. (2014, September 27). *What makes mothers kill their own children?* Retrieved July 6, 2015, from Washington Post: http://www.washingtonpost.com/local/what-makes-mothers-kill-their-children/2014/09/27/f599f0b4-4018-11e4-b03f-de718edeb92f_story.html

Lacayo, R. (2001, December 3). About Face for Afghan Women. *Time Magazine*. Retrieved from
http://www.time.com/time/world/article/0,8599,185651,00.html

Lagerspetz, K. M., Bjorqvist, K., & Peltonen, T. (1988). Is Indirect Aggression More Typical of Females? Gender Differences in Aggressiveness in 11 and 12-Year Old Children. *Aggressive Behavior, 14*, 403-414.

Layton, J. (2006, August 29). *What causes Stockholm syndrome?* Retrieved September 29, 2014, from How Stuff Works: http://health.howstuffworks.com/mental-health/mental-disorders/stockholm-syndrome.htm

Lilienfeld, S. O., & Arkowitz, H. (2010, April 5). Are Men the More Belligerent Sex? *Scientific American*, p. 2. Retrieved from http://www.scientificamerican.com/article.cfm?id=are-men-the-more-belligerent-sex

Lunchboxcafe. (2013, November 28). *Black Friday - 2013 Wal Mart*. Retrieved May 15, 2016, from [YouTube]: http://youtu.be/ucrM3TLLJRs

McElroy, W. (2002, January 29). *FOXNews.com: Are Fathers' Rights a Factor in Male Suicide?* Retrieved April 17, 2006, from FOXNews.com: http://www.foxnews.com/story/0,2933,44183,00.html

Mehraspand, A. (2013, December 6). *Indentured servitude for men in Iran: The myth of patriarchal oppressive divorce*. Retrieved January 17, 2014, from A Voice for Men: http://www.avoiceformen.com/feminism/feminist-lies-feminism/indentured-servitude-for-men-in-iran-the-myth-of-patriarchal-oppressive-divorce/

Merrick, B. R. (2014, April 29). *On Feminism's Infantalization of Women*. Retrieved August 17, 2014, from A Voice for Men:

http://www.avoiceformen.com/gynocentrism/on-feminisms-infantilization-of-women/

Milner, L. S. (1998). *A Brief History of Infanticide.* Retrieved July 6, 2015, from The Society for the Prevention of Infanticide: http://www.infanticide.org/history.htm

Mina, D. (2003, January 13). *Why Are Women Drawn to Men Behind Bars?* Retrieved January 30, 2013, from The Guardian: http://www.guardian.co.uk/world/2003/jan/13/gender.uk

Mirrlees-Black, C. (1999). *Domestic Violence: Findings from a new British Crime Survey self-completion questionnaire.* London: Home Office. Retrieved from: http://webarchive.nationalarchives.gov.uk/20110218135832/rds.homeoffice.gov.uk/rds/pdfs/hors191.pdf

Molyneux, S. (2009, December 15). *The Bomb in the Brain Part 1 - The True Roots of Human Violence.* Retrieved August 7, 2012, from Freedomain Radio: http://www.youtube.com/watch?v=gbiq2-ukfhM

Molyneux, S. (2013, November 6). *The Truth About Violence - The facts will shock you.* Retrieved January 17, 2014, from Stefan Molyneux [YouTube]: https://youtu.be/Pw_UlUGoUV4?list=PLMNj_r5bccUyulYsatrzNGIvasrOeBy_Y

Nin, A. (1970). *The Diary of Anaïs Nin, Vol. 2: 1934-1939* (1970 ed.). (G. Stuhlmann, Ed.) Boston: Mariner Books.

Norma, C., & Tankard Reist, M. (Eds.). (2016). *Prostitution Narratives: Stories of Survival in the Sex Trade.* North Melbourne, Victoria, Australia: Spinifex Press Pty Ltd.

O'Brien, N. (2005, November 15). Mum's Permission Needed for Terror Plan. *The Australian*, p. 1.

O'Hara, R. (2013, September 20). *Circumcision in Africa not preventing HIV.* Retrieved January 17, 2014, from A Voice for Men: http://www.avoiceformen.com/updates/circumcision-in-africa-not-preventing-spread-of-hiv/

Oliver, A. (2012, September 23). *Imelda Marcos' famous collection of 3,000 shoes partly destroyed by termites and floods.* Retrieved May 15, 2016, from Daily Mail: http://www.dailymail.co.uk/news/article-2207353/Imelda-Marcos-legendary-3-000-plus-shoe-collection-destroyed-termites-floods-neglect.html

Oltermann, P. (2014, February 2). *Female defence ministers pledge to break Europe's old boys' network.* Retrieved May 13, 2016, from The Guardian: http://www.theguardian.com/world/2014/feb/02/female-defence-ministers-tweet-photograph

Panarchy.org. (2012, November 24). *Ludwig von Bertalanffy - passages from General System Theory (1968).* (G. P. De Bellis, Ed.) Retrieved

January 6, 2013, from Panarchy-Panarchie-Panarchia-Panarquia: http://www.panarchy.org/vonbertalanffy/systems.1968.html

Peck, S. (1978). *The Road Less Traveled: A New Psychology of Love, Traditional Values and Spiritual Growth.* Simon & Schuster.

Peirce, C. S. (1931-1966). *Collected Papers of Charles Sanders Peirce, 8 vols.* (C. Hartshorne, P. Weiss, & A. W. Burks, Eds.) Cambridge, MA: Harvard University Press.

Pirsig, R. M. (1974). *Zen and the Art of Motorcycle Maintenance: An Inquiry Into Values.* New York: Bantam Books.

Pope Paul VI. (1968, July 25). *Humanae Vitae (On the Regulation of Human Births), Encyclical of Pope Paul VI.* Retrieved December 4, 2012, from Papal Encyclicals Online: http://www.papalencyclicals.net/Paul06/p6humana.htm

Quote Garden. (2010, September 9). *Habit quotes, sayings about good and bad habits.* Retrieved January 3, 2013, from http://www.quotegarden.com/habits.html

Sapozhnikova, G. (2008, June 25). Russian and Austrian sex maniacs share shocking similarities. *KP.RU.* Retrieved July 20, 2016, from http://www.kp.ru/daily/24119/341715/

Schneider, W. H. (2004, May 1). *Fathers for Life.* Retrieved May 1, 2004, from Fathers for Life: http://www.fathersforlife.org/ussuic.htm

Sewell, S., & Sewell, B. (2000). *Report on Family Violence.* Retrieved 2000, from Family Resources and Research: http://mywebpages.comcast.net/ssewell38/Family-Violence.htm

Shapiro, F. R. (1985, March 20). Historical Notes on the Vocabulary of the Women's Movement. *American Speech, 60*(1), 3-16. Retrieved from http://www.jstor.org/discover/10.2307/454643?uid=3737536&uid=2&uid=4&sid=21101677023673

Shatz, C. J. (1992, September). The developing brain. *Scientific American: Mind and Brain, 267*(3), pp. 35-41.

Simmons, R. (2002). *Odd Girl Out: The Hidden Culture of Aggression in Girls.* Harcourt, Inc.

Siteclopedia: Salem Witch Trials. (2000, July 8). *Salem Witch Trials.* Retrieved April 17, 2006, from Siteclopedia: http://www.salemwitchtrials.com/index.html

Smith, S. (2004, May 1). Women and Islam. (A. Shawki, Ed.) *International Socialist Review*(35). Retrieved January 24, 2013, from International Socialist Review, Issue 35: http://www.isreview.org/issues/35/women_islam.shtml

Solway, K. (n.d.). *The main parts of Sex and Character, by Otto Weininger.* Retrieved February 27, 2013, from The Absolute - truth, thinking, philosophy, genius: http://www.theabsolute.net/ottow/sexcharh.html

Sotomayor, T. (2013, January 22). *Woman Calls Thugs To Shoot Up Bus After Argument With Passenger.* Retrieved September 29, 2014, from Tommy Sotomayor [YouTube]: http://youtu.be/LiH2dUFv43Y

Stamm, J. (2007, September 22). *PPE Connections - Fall 2007.* Retrieved December 30, 2012, from PPE Connections: http://www.newdirectionsinstitute.org/documents/PPEConnecti onsFall2007.pdf

Stamm, J., & Spencer, P. (2007). *Bright from the start: The simple, science-backed way to nurture your child's developing mind from birth to age 3* (2007 ed.). New York: Gotham Books. Retrieved December 30, 2012, from http://www.brightfromthestartthebook.com/index.php

Steinmetz, S. K. (1981). A Cross Cultural Comparison of Marital Abuse. *Journal of Sociology and Social Welfare, 8,* 404-414.

Straus, M. A., & Gelles, R. J. (1986). Societal Change and Change in Family Violence from 1975 to 1985 as Revealed by Two National Surveys. *Journal of Marriage and the Family, 48*(3), 465-479.

Straus, M. A., Gelles, R. J., & Steinmetz, S. K. (1980). *Behind Closed Doors: Violence in the American Family* (1980 ed.). New York: Doubleday.

Sukel, K. (2012). *Dirty Minds: How Our Brains Influence Love, Sex, and Relationships.* New York: Free Press (Simon & Schuster).

The Oatmeal. (n.d.). *How the male angler fish gets completely screwed.* Retrieved January 03, 2013, from http://theoatmeal.com/comics/angler

Tieman, A. (2014, January 13). *Men's Rights versus Feminism explained using magnets.* Retrieved June 8, 2014, from A Voice for Men: http://www.youtube.com/watch?v=PF_WLlMWk6U

Tomassi, R. (2016, May 6). *Category archives: Hypergamy.* Retrieved May 15, 2016, from The Rational Male: http://therationalmale.com/category/hypergamy-2/

Tomassi, R. (2020). *The Rational Male - Religion.* Reno, Nevada: Counterflow Media.

University of California, Davis. (2017, June 15). *Close-up view of DNA replication yields surprises.* Retrieved February 7, 2021, from EurekAlert!: https://www.eurekalert.org/pub_releases/2017-06/uoc--vio061317.php

Unmasking feminism. (2010). *Remove the needs (repost from 2010).* Retrieved January 19, 2014, from http://unmaskingfeminism.wordpress.com/2013/11/22/remove-the-needs-repost-from-2010/

Urban Dictionary. (2012, June 5). *Rationalization hamster.* Retrieved July 18, 2015, from Urban Dictionary: http://www.urbandictionary.com/define.php?term=rationalizatio n+hamster

Von Glinow, K. (2012, July 11). *Mick Jagger Sex Life: Rocker Has Slept With 4,000 Women, Biographer Says.* Retrieved January 7, 2013, from Huffington Post - Huffpost Celebrity: http://www.huffingtonpost.com/2012/07/11/mick-jagger-sex-life-4000-women_n_1666176.html

Weininger, O. (1906). *Sex and character* (6 ed.). London & New York: William Heinemann & G.P. Putnam's Sons. Retrieved from http://www.theabsolute.net/ottow/sexcharh.html

Weininger, O. (1906). *Sex and character* (Translated from the 6th German edition ed.). London, New York: London: William Heinemann. New York: G.P. Putnam's Sons. Retrieved from http://www.theabsolute.net/ottow/sexcharh.html

Wex Legal Dictionary. (n.d.). *Equal Protection.* Retrieved May 15, 2016, from https://www.law.cornell.edu/wex/equal_protection

Wikipedia - Angler fish. (2012, December 20). *Anglerfish.* Retrieved January 3, 2013, from Wikipedia: http://en.wikipedia.org/wiki/Anglerfish

Wikipedia - Charles Sanders Peirce. (2012, December 6). *Charles Sanders Peirce.* Retrieved January 3, 2013, from Wikipedia: http://en.wikipedia.org/wiki/Charles_Sanders_Peirce

Wikipedia - Don Giovanni. (2012, November 29). *Don Giovanni.* Retrieved December 6, 2012, from Wikipedia: http://en.wikipedia.org/wiki/Don_Giovanni

Wikipedia - Evolutionary Psychology. (2013, June 2). *Evolutionary Psychology.* Retrieved June 4, 2013, from Wikipedia: http://en.wikipedia.org/wiki/Evolutionary_psychology

Wikipedia - Gerald Edelman. (2012, December 16). *Wikipedia.* Retrieved January 6, 2013, from Gerald Edelman: http://en.wikipedia.org/wiki/Gerald_Edelman

Wikipedia - Giacomo Casanova. (2012, December 1). *Giacomo Casanova.* Retrieved December 6, 2012, from Wikipedia: http://en.wikipedia.org/wiki/Giacomo_Casanova

Wikipedia - Memetics. (2012, December 5). *Memetics.* Retrieved January 3, 2013, from Wikipedia: http://en.wikipedia.org/wiki/Memetics

Wikipedia - Pragmatism. (2013, January 5). *Wikipedia.* Retrieved January 7, 2013, from Pragmatism:http://en.wikipedia.org/wiki/Pragmatism

Wikipedia - Sexual dimorphism. (2012, December 26). *sexual dimorphism.* Retrieved January 3, 2013, from Wikipedia: http://en.wikipedia.org/wiki/Sexual_dimorphism

Wikipedia - Systems theory. (2012, December 15). *Systems theory.* Retrieved January 6, 2013, from Wikipedia: http://en.wikipedia.org/wiki/Systems_theory

Wikipedia - Theodore Lidz. (2012, April 8). *Theodore Lidz*. Retrieved August 7, 2012, from Wikipedia, The Free Encyclopedia: http://en.wikipedia.org/wiki/Theodore_Lidz

Wikipedia. (2013, October 28). *Complexity theory*. Retrieved January 20, 2014, from Wikipedia, The Free Encyclopedia: http://en.wikipedia.org/wiki/Complexity_theory

Wikipedia. (2013, November 14). *Relational aggression*. Retrieved January 17, 2014, from Wikipedia, The Free Encyclopedia: http://en.wikipedia.org/wiki/Relational_aggression

Wikipedia. (2014, January 9). *Neuroplasticity*. Retrieved January 17, 2014, from Wikipedia, The Free Encyclopedia: http://en.wikipedia.org/wiki/Neuroplasticity

Wikipedia. (2014, January 15). *Polygyny*. Retrieved January 20, 2014, from Wikipedia, The Free Encyclopedia: http://en.wikipedia.org/wiki/Polygyny

Wikipedia. (2016, July 16). *Feral child*. Retrieved July 21, 2016, from Wikipedia, The Free Encyclopedia: https://en.wikipedia.org/wiki/Feral_child

Woods, B. (Director). (1995). *The Dying Rooms Trust* [Motion Picture]. United Kingdom. Retrieved August 1, 2002, from http://www.dmcl.com/dying-rooms/page1.htm

World Health Organization. (2013, February). *Female genital mutilation - Fact sheet No 241*. Retrieved January 17, 2014, from WHO: http://www.who.int/mediacentre/factsheets/fs241/en/

Yanega, D. (2006, November 2). *Entemology (Study of bugs): Fly size VS Human*. Retrieved from Expert Archive Questions: http://experts.about.com/q/Entomology-Study-Bugs-665/Fly-size-VS-Human.htm

Yeager, J. (2019, February 1). *Hot Crazy Matrix A Man's Guide to Women - ORIGINAL*. Retrieved September 7, 2020, from Youtube: https://youtu.be/pInk1rV2VEg

Zimmer, C. (2012, April 16). *A Sharp Rise in Retractions Prompts Calls for Reform*. Retrieved February 17, 2013, from New York Times: http://www.nytimes.com/2012/04/17/science/rise-in-scientific-journal-retractions-prompts-calls-for-reform.html?pagewanted=all

Zohrab, P. (2011, January 9). *The Frontman Fallacy, Feminism, and Men's Rights*. Retrieved February 8, 2013, from The Black Ribbon Campaign: Combatting Feminist Lies: http://peterzohrab.tripod.com/frontman.html

# GLOSSARY

**Beta orbiter:** A male who invests time and effort nurturing friendships with women in the hope of eventually getting into a relationship or having sex with them. They often don't mind being friend-zoned, accepting it as the cost of doing business; indeed patience for those who are friend-zoned can sometimes yield the desired outcome.

**Determinism (also genocentric determinism):** Emphasizes bottom-up direction of causation, as opposed to top-down. Other terms that relate include *reductionism*, and *linear reductionism*. Generally, the assumption is that genes determine phenotypic traits, whether morphological or behavioural, to the exclusion of environmental influences. More recent developments include *epigenetics*, which factors in the environment in influencing which genes are expressed. But ultimately *epigenetics* has not escaped the narrative of determinism because its emphasis remains genocentric (of genetic, bottom-up causation).

**Domestic violence:** Acronyms associated with the *domestic violence* industry include:
- DV – domestic violence;
- VAWA – Violence Against Woman Act (USA).

**Evolutionary psychology (EP):** From Wikipedia(Evolutionary Psychology, 2013), *"Evolutionary psychology (EP) is an approach in the social and natural sciences that examines psychological traits such as memory, perception, and language from a modern evolutionary perspective. It seeks to identify which human psychological traits are evolved adaptations – that is, the functional products of natural selection or sexual selection."*

**Game:** Usually associated with the seduction community as a toolkit of techniques for seducing women. The terminology most often associated with *Game* establishes its shallow priorities directed at manipulating women. For example:

- *PUA* - Pick-up artist;
- *Negs* - Narratives designed to lower a woman's self-esteem for the purpose of facilitating seduction. It has to be done subtly, perhaps good-naturedly and with a sense of humour whilst demonstrating high mate value – putting a woman down as a means of disarming her. As with other aspects of *Game*, it has to be done without her being aware that she is being manipulated;
- *Social proof* - Game harnesses women's proclivity to social indicators of status, such as the company that a man keeps, and his status within his group. Hence the emergence of terms that rank men in an hierarchical pecking order, like *alpha* (dominant male), *beta* (usually subordinate to the alpha) and *omega* (submissive male of low mate value).

But ultimately *Game* is not a new concept and not always based in shallow motives. *PUA Game* is a rather recent innovation, but its more authentic antecedents might be recognized in the traditions of what it means to be a man – for example, in rites of passage, or in fathers teaching their sons codes of honor, respectability, courage. The *PUA*-inspired idea that men must make like performing seals in order to impress women is a rather recent innovation (relating to the emergence of feminism and our contraceptive technologies along with the theoretical implications of EP) that is in stark contrast to the older traditions of masculinity, with its own integrity, that never felt as though it owed anyone an apology. We anticipate contemporary *PUA Game*, like feminism, to have a short self-life, given the absence of solid values to sustain it.

**Genocentrism (genocentric):** The presumption that genes determine phenotypic traits, whether morphological or behavioural. This is the neo-Darwinian interpretation of evolution, where mutations are said to provide the basis for adaptive traits in natural selection.

**Gynocentrism (gynocentric)**: Gynocentrism refers to the cultural narrative that emphasizes women's status, perspectives and priorities. Feminism is one manifestation of gynocentric culture. Some authors attribute gynocentrism's origins to feudalism in medieval Europe. The perspective taken in this book, however, is that gynocentrism is more general than that, beginning first as a natural predisposition to defer to the matriarchal authority of the primary nurturer. All cultures must, to a greater or lesser extent, contend with gynocentrism, just as within every culture exists both matriarchal and patriarchal dimensions of authority.

**Hypergamy:** The practice of "marrying up." In western and most other cultures, this manifests in women's preferences for the most successful, or dominant men, where said success/dominance is established in parameters such as education, social status, career advancement, or capital accumulation. Depending on the culture, other variations on the *hypergamy* theme might relate to things like courage, victories in battle or creative talents. By contrast, particularly in the contemporary west, men's preferences for women are based principally in physical appearance.

**Incel:** Elliot Rodger's shooting of six people in 2014 first drew media attention to the concept of involuntary celibacy. *Incel* relates to an online community where members define themselves as unable to find romantic or sexual partners, despite desiring one. The term relates to both men and women, and the first incel website, Alana's Involuntary Celibacy Project, was established by a woman. However, the term has more recently come to be associated with the manosphere, MGTOW and the men's rights movement.

**Initial conditions (chaos theory, complex adaptive systems):** Within the narrative of dynamic systems, initial conditions relate to the seed values that impact critically on the future developmental trajectory of the system.

**Lamarckism:** In Lamarckism, or Lamarckian adaptation, an organism acquires characteristics through use or disuse throughout its life, and passes on these characteristics to its offspring. The classic example of Lamarckism that is often cited in the literature is the giraffe's long neck.

**Liberalism:** In Australia, liberals are identified as conservatives, while the left is associated with Labor. As this book is directed at a global audience, any reference to *liberal* is made in the context of *American liberal...* that is, the left that is associated with the US Democrats.

**Mind-body unity**: The relationship between *mind* and *body* is an important one that is of increasing relevance in *semiotics, biosemiotics, cognitive science* and *neuroplasticity*. Indeed, it is impossible to understand cognitive processes without understanding the relationship between *mind* and *body*. The *mind-body* relationship is important to understanding human sexuality and gender roles. It is beyond the scope of this book to delve into these theoretical concepts in detail, but the reader is encouraged to do further research into an area that holds all the promise of a new kind of Copernican revolution.

**Men's Rights Movement (MRM)**: Acronyms associated with the men's rights movement include:
- *MGTOW* - Men going their own way;
- *MRA* - Men's rights activist;
- *MHRA* – Men's human rights activist.

**Phenotype, phenotypic**: These are the observable physical or biochemical characteristics of an organism, as determined by both genetic makeup (genotype) and environmental adaptive pressures (natural selection).

**Red pill versus blue pill – The Matrix:** We will often find references in MRA/MHRA literature to the *red pill* and the *blue pill*. In the popular science fiction movie The Matrix, the main character Neo has to choose between the *red pill* and the *blue pill*. The *blue pill* would enable Neo to continue with the fabricated reality of the Matrix (in our case, feminism), whereas the *red pill* would enable him to escape from the Matrix and into the real world (AVfM, men's rights).

# NOTES TO CHAPTERS

## NOTES TO CHAPTER 1 – THEORETICAL OUTLINE

[1] Jarosek, S. (2013). Pragmatism, neural plasticity and mind-body unity. *Biosemiotics, 6*(2), 205-230. Retrieved from http://link.springer.com/article/10.1007%2Fs12304-012-9145-5

[2] Doidge, N. (2008). *The Brain that Changes Itself* (2008 ed.). Melbourne: Scribe Publications. Retrieved 12 6, 2012, from:
http://www.normandoidge.com/normandoidge.com/MAIN.html

[3] Jarosek, S. (2013). Pragmatism, neural plasticity and mind-body unity. *Biosemiotics, 6*(2), 205-230. Retrieved from http://link.springer.com/article/10.1007%2Fs12304-012-9145-5

[4] Coach Red Pill. (2020, August 11). *Treat a woman like a nerd.* Retrieved March 7, 2020, from Coach Red Pill [YouTube]: https://youtu.be/EGKpS1wVqL8

## NOTES TO CHAPTER 2 – IN THE SERVICE OF CULTURE'S QUEEN BEE

[1] Wikipedia - Sexual dimorphism, 2012. http://en.wikipedia.org/wiki/Sexual_dimorphism.

[2] Quote Garden, 2010. Habit quotes, sayings about good and bad habits:
http://www.quotegarden.com/habits.html

[3] Green, 2007. The Principles of Psychology, William James (1890)- Chapter IV, Habit:
http://psychclassics.yorku.ca/James/Principles/prin4.htm

[4] Wikipedia - Charles Sanders Peirce, 2012. Charles Sanders Peirce:
http://en.wikipedia.org/wiki/Charles_Sanders_Peirce

[5] Anomalistic Psychology Research Unit (APRU), 2009. Morphic Resonance, Collective Memory and the Habits of Nature: http://vimeo.com/11653660

[6] Wikipedia - Memetics, 2012. Memetics: http://en.wikipedia.org/wiki/Memetics

[7] The Oatmeal, n.d. How the male angler fish gets completely screwed:
http://theoatmeal.com/comics/angler

[8] Wikipedia - Angler fish, 2012. Anglerfish: http://en.wikipedia.org/wiki/Anglerfish

[9] Wikipedia - Systems theory, 2012. Systems theory:
http://en.wikipedia.org/wiki/Systems_theory

[10] Panarchy.org, 2012. Ludwig von Bertalanffy - passages from General System Theory (1968): http://www.panarchy.org/vonbertalanffy/systems.1968.html

[11] Doidge, N., 2008. The Brain that Changes Itself. Melbourne: Scribe Publications:
http://www.normandoidge.com/normandoidge.com/MAIN.html

[12] Wikipedia - Gerald Edelman, 2012. Wikipedia:
http://en.wikipedia.org/wiki/Gerald_Edelman

[13] Doidge, N., 2008. The Brain that Changes Itself. Melbourne: Scribe Publications:
http://www.normandoidge.com/normandoidge.com/MAIN.html

[14] Anon., n.d. Facts on Fatherless Kids:
http://www.photius.com/feminocracy/facts_on_fatherless_kids.html

[15] Administration for Children & Families, 2002. Child Maltreatment 2002:
http://archive.acf.hhs.gov/programs/cb/pubs/cm02/cm02.pdf

[16] Wikipedia - Pragmatism, 2013. Wikipedia: http://en.wikipedia.org/wiki/Pragmatism

17 Shatz, C. J., 1992. The developing brain. Scientific American: Mind and Brain, September, 267(3), pp. 35-41.

18 Cherry, K., n.d. What Is Brain Plasticity?:
http://psychology.about.com/od/biopsychology/f/brain-plasticity.htm

19 Molyneux, S., 2009. The Bomb in the Brain Part 1 - The True Roots of Human Violence:
http://www.youtube.com/watch?v=gbiq2-ukfhM

20 Molyneux, S. (2013, November 6). The Truth About Violence - The facts will shock you. [Youtube]. Retrieved January 17, 2014, from https://youtu.be/Pw_UlUGoUV4?list=PLMNj_r5bccUyulYsatrzNGIvasrOeBy_Y

21 Molyneux, S., 2009. The Bomb in the Brain Part 1 - The True Roots of Human Violence:
http://www.youtube.com/watch?v=gbiq2-ukfhM

22 Stamm, J., 2007. PPE Connections - Fall 2007:
http://www.newdirectionsinstitute.org/documents/PPEConnectionsFall2007.pdf

23 Stamm, J. & Spencer, P., 2007. Bright from the start: The simple, science-backed way to nurture your child's developing mind from birth to age 3. 2007 ed. New York: Gotham Books.

24 cbresearch, 2007. The Baby Brain Box / Dr. Jill Stamm Interview:
http://www.youtube.com/watch?v=baek--_1ZfU

25 Sapozhnikova, G., 2008. Russian and Austrian sex maniacs share shocking similarities. KP.RU, 25 June: http://www.kp.ru/daily/24119/341715/

26 Connolly, K., 2009. Fritzl's troubled childhood analysed in court. The Guardian, 18 March: http://www.guardian.co.uk/world/2009/mar/18/psychiatrist-analyses-josef-fritzl

27 Peck, S., 1978. The Road Less Traveled: A New Psychology of Love, Traditional Values and Spiritual Growth. s.l.:Simon & Schuster.

28 Wikipedia - Theodore Lidz, 2012. Theodore Lidz:
http://en.wikipedia.org/wiki/Theodore_Lidz

29 Harrington, A., 2012. The fall of the schizophrenogenic mother -. The Lancet, 7 April, 379(9823), pp. 1292-1293:
http://www.thelancet.com/journals/lancet/article/PIIS0140-6736(12)60546-7/fulltext

30 Haier, R. J. et al., 2005. The neuroanatomy of general intelligence: sex matters. NeuroImage, 25, 320-327.. NeuroImage, Volume 25, pp. 320-327.

31 Hutson, M., 2008. Why Do Women Have Erotic Rape Fantasies?:
http://www.psychologytoday.com/blog/psyched/200805/why-do-women-have-erotic-rape-fantasies

32 Weininger, O., 1906. Sex and character. Translated from the 6th German edition ed. London, New York: London: William Heinemann. New York: G.P. Putnam's Sons:
http://www.theabsolute.net/ottow/sexcharh.html

33 Solway, K., n.d. The main parts of Sex and Character, by Otto Weininger:
http://www.theabsolute.net/ottow/sexcharh.html

34 Chateau Heartiste, 2012. More scientific evidence that chicks dig jerks:
http://heartiste.wordpress.com/2012/06/15/more-scientific-evidence-that-chicks-dig-jerks/

35 Sukel, K., 2012. Dirty Minds: How Our Brains Influence Love, Sex, and Relationships. New York: Free Press (Simon & Schuster).

36 Kshatriya, R., 2012. The ineffable mystery of Anglo hypergamy: http://kshatriya-anglobitch.blogspot.com.au/2012/10/the-ineffable-mystery-of-anglo-hypergamy.html

37 Von Glinow, K., 2012. Mick Jagger Sex Life: Rocker Has Slept With 4,000 Women, Biographer Says: http://www.huffingtonpost.com/2012/07/11/mick-jagger-sex-life-4000-women_n_1666176.html

[38] Factory, 2011. Answering a schoolgirl's questions:
http://www.avoiceformen.com/feminism/answering-a-schoolgirls-questions/
[39] Shapiro, F. R., 1985. Historical Notes on the Vocabulary of the Women's Movement. American Speech, 20 March, 60(1), pp. 3-16.

**NOTES TO CHAPTER 3 – MATRIARCHAL OPPRESSION IN CULTURE**

[1] Baskerville, S., 1999. Why is daddy in jail?. The Women's Quarterly, no. 18, Winter, 1999, 22 December, Issue 18.
[2] Merrick, B. R. (2014, April 29). On Feminism's Infantalization of Women. *A Voice for Men*. Retrieved August 17, 2014, from http://www.avoiceformen.com/gynocentrism/on-feminisms-infantilization-of-women/
[3] Lagerspetz, K. M., Bjorqvist, K. & Peltonen, T., 1988. Is Indirect Aggression More Typical of Females? Gender Differences in Aggressiveness in 11 and 12-Year Old Children. Aggressive Behavior, Volume 14, pp. 403-414.
[4] Bjorqvist, K., 1994. Sex Differences in Physical, Verbal and Indirect Aggression: A Review of Recent Research. Sex Roles: A Journal of Research, Volume 30, pp. 177-188.
[5] Crick, N. R., 1995. Relational Aggression: The Role of Intent Attributions, Feelings of Distress, and Provocation Type. Development and Psychopathology, Volume 7, pp. 313-322.
[6] Crick, N. R. & Grotpeter, J. K., 1995. Relational Aggression, Gender, and Social-Psychological Adjustment. Child Development, Volume 66, pp. 710-722.
[7] Simmons, R., 2002. Odd Girl Out: The Hidden Culture of Aggression in Girls. s.l.:Harcourt, Inc..
[8] Chesler, P., 2001. Woman's inhumanity to woman. New York: Thunder's Mouth Press/Nation Books.
[9] Weininger, O., 1906. Sex and character. Translated from the 6th German edition ed. London, New York: London: William Heinemann. New York: G.P. Putnam's Sons.
[10] Pirsig, R. M., 1974. Zen and the Art of Motorcycle Maintenance: An Inquiry Into Values. New York: Bantam Books.
[11] Chesler, Phyllis. *Woman's Inhumanity to Woman:* 93.
[12] Jarosek, S. (2013). Pragmatism, neural plasticity and mind-body unity. *Biosemiotics, 6*(2), 205-230.
[13] Feral child. (2016, July 16). In *Wikipedia, The Free Encyclopedia*. Retrieved July 21, 2016, from: https://en.wikipedia.org/wiki/Feral_child
[14] Merrick, B. R. (2014, April 29). On Feminism's Infantalization of Women. *A Voice for Men*. Retrieved August 17, 2014, from http://www.avoiceformen.com/gynocentrism/on-feminisms-infantilization-of-women/
[15] Layton, J. What causes Stockholm syndrome? *How Stuff Works*. Retrieved September 29, 2014, from http://health.howstuffworks.com/mental-health/mental-disorders/stockholm-syndrome.htm
[16] Canetti, E. (1973). *Crowds and Power*. Penguin Books.
[17] Amnesty International, n.d. Female genital mutilation:
http://www.amnesty.org/ailib/intcam/femgen/fgm1.htm
[18] FGC Education and Networking Project, 2003. Facing Mt. Kenya - Jomo Kenyatta:
http://www.fgmnetwork.org/articles/kenyatta/index.html
[19] Kenyatta, J., 1965. Facing Mt. Kenya. 1965 ed. New York: Vintage Books.
[20] Siteclopedia: Salem Witch Trials, 2000. Salem Witch Trials:
http://www.salemwitchtrials.com/index.html

[21] Smith, S., 2004. Women and Islam. International Socialist Review, 1 May.Issue 35.

[22] Lacayo, R., 2001. About Face for Afghan Women. Time Magazine, 3 December.

[23] Gendercide Watch website - http://www.gendercide.org/ As in March 2003. Adam Jones is the Executive Director of Gendercide Watch, and Editor of "Gendercide and Genocide".

[24] Gendercide Watch website on witchhunts - http://www.gendercide.org/case_witchhunts.html.

[25] Milner, L. S. (1998). A Brief History of Infanticide. *The Society for the Prevention of Infanticide.* Retrieved July 6, 2015, from http://www.infanticide.org/history.htm

[26] Kunkle, F. (2014, September 27). What makes mothers kill their own children? *Washington Post.* Retrieved July 6, 2015, from http://www.washingtonpost.com/local/what-makes-mothers-kill-their-children/2014/09/27/f599f0b4-4018-11e4-b03f-de718edeb92f_story.html

[27] Gendercide Watch website on infanticide - http://www.gendercide.org/case_infanticide.html.

[28] Woods, Brian (producer). *The Dying Rooms.* True Vision, 1995. Website from the "The Dying Rooms Trust" - http://www.dmcl.com/dying-rooms/page1.htm. As on August 1, 2002.

[29] Beckett, F. (2008, November 11). First world war: The men who would not fight. Retrieved February 08, 2021, from The Guardian: https://www.theguardian.com/world/2008/nov/11/first-world-war-white-feather-cowardice

[30] Gullace, N. (2014, June 30). The 'White Feather Girls': Women's militarism in the UK. Retrieved February 08, 2021, from openDemocracy: https://www.opendemocracy.net/en/5050/white-feather-girls-womens-militarism-in-uk/

[31] Angelucci, Marc and Glenn Sacks. "Research Shows False Accusations of Rape Common." Appearing in the *Los Angeles Daily Journal* and *San Francisco Daily Journal.* September 15, 2004. Glenn Sacks website - http://www.glennjsacks.com/research_shows_false.htm

[32] 60 Minutes Australia, reporter Richard Carlton. *Human Bombs.* Channel 9, August 19, 2001 - http://sixtyminutes.ninemsn.com.au/article/258824/human-bombs

[33] O'Brien, Natalie. "Mum's Permission Needed for Terror Plan." *The Australian,* November 15, 2005.

[34] Administration for Children and Families. *Child Maltreatment 2002.* Department of Health and Human Services, Washington, D.C., 2002. Based on data collected via the National Child Abuse and Neglect Data System (NCANDS). National Clearinghouse on Child Abuse and Neglect Information - Original data obtained from: http://www.calib.com/nccanch/faq.cfm. Child Maltreant 2002 report downloaded from: http://www.acf.hhs.gov/programs/cb/stats_research/index.htm. As on April 28, 2006.

[35] Ibid.: 61, 63.

[36] Ibid.: 66.

[37] Ibid.: 52.

[38] Administration for Children & Families, 2012. Child Maltreatment 2011: http://www.acf.hhs.gov/programs/cb/resource/child-maltreatment-2011

[39] Elam, P. 2011, March 26. Mary kellett: This time it's for real. Retrieved February 08, 2021, from https://avoiceformen.com/government-tyranny/mary-kellett-this-time-its-for-real/

[40] Baskerville, S., 1999. Why is daddy in jail?. The Women's Quarterly, no. 18, Winter, 1999, 22 December, Issue 18.

[41] Chesler, Phyllis. *Woman's Inhumanity to Woman.* 254.

[42] Ibid.: 255.

[43] Ibid.: 263.

[44] Ibid.: 264.

[45] Ibid.: 267.

[46] Mina, Denise. "Why Are Women Drawn to Men Behind Bars?" *The Guardian,* January 13, 2003 - http://www.guardian.co.uk/world/2003/jan/13/gender.uk. As on January 30, 2013.

[47] Isenberg, Sheila. *Women Who Love Men Who Kill.* iUniverse, 2000.

[48] Castleman, M., 2010. All about sex: Women's rape fantasies: How common? What do they mean?: http://www.psychologytoday.com/blog/all-about-sex/201001/womens-rape-fantasies-how-common-what-do-they-mean

[49] Hutson, M., 2008. Why Do Women Have Erotic Rape Fantasies?: http://www.psychologytoday.com/blog/psyched/200805/why-do-women-have-erotic-rape-fantasies

[50] Nin, A., 1970. The Diary of Anaïs Nin, Vol. 2: 1934-1939. 1970 ed. Boston: Mariner Books.

[51] Fiebert, Martin S. *References examining assaults by women on their spouses or male partners: an annotated bibliography,* 2005. Portions of this paper were presented at the American Psychological Society Convention in Washington, D.C. May 24, 1997. Earlier versions of this paper appeared in Sexuality and Culture 1 (1997): 273-286, and Sexuality and Culture 8:3-4 (2004): 140-177 -http://www.csulb.edu/~mfiebert/assault.htm. As on April 17, 2006.

[52] Lilienfeld, S. O. & Arkowitz, H., 2010. Are Men the More Belligerent Sex?. Scientific American, 5 April, p. 2.

[53] British Crime Survey 1996. Catriona Mirrlees-Black. Home Office Research Study, 1999.

[54] Crick, N.R. and Grotpeter, J.K. "Relational Aggression, Gender, and Social-Psychological Adjustment." *Child Development* 66 (1995): 710-722.

[55] Straus, Murray A., Richard J. Gelles and Suzanne K. Steinmetz. *Behind Closed Doors: Violence in the American Family.* Doubleday, 1980: 36.

[56] Straus, Murray A. and Richard J. Gelles. "Societal Change and Change in Family Violence from 1975 to 1985 as Revealed by Two National Surveys." *Journal of Marriage and the Family* 48:3 (1986): 465-479.

[57] Steinmetz, Suzanne K. "A Cross Cultural Comparison of Marital Abuse." *Journal of Sociology and Social Welfare* 8 (1981): 404-414.

[58] Archer, John. "Sex Differences in Aggression Between Heterosexual Partners: A Meta-Analytic Review." *Psychological Bulletin* 136:5 (2000) 651-680.

[59] Sewell, Reverends Sam and Bunny. Report on Family Violence. Originally hosted on website (Family Resources and Research): http://mywebpages.comcast.net/ssewell38/Family-Violence.htm

[60] John the Other, 2012. Violence by proxy: http://www.avoiceformen.com/feminism/government-tyranny/violence-by-proxy/

[61] Sotomayor, T. (2013, January 22). Woman Calls Thugs To Shoot Up Bus After Argument With Passenger. [Youtube]. Retrieved September 29, 2014, from http://youtu.be/LiH2dUFv43Y

[62] In its original form, this topic was published as an article in the July/August edition (2004) of Transitions, by the National Coalition of Free Men

[63] Furchtgott-Roth, Diana and Christine Stolba. *Women's Figures: An Illustrated Guide to the Economic Progress of Women in America.* American Enterprise Institute, 1999.

[64] Belkin, Lisa. "The Opt-Out Revolution." *New York Times,* October 26, 2003 - http://www.nytimes.com/2003/10/26/magazine/26WOMEN.html

[65] Allen, Charlotte. "Return of the Guy." *We Love Guys.* Independent Women's Forum, May 3, 2003 - http://www.iwf.org/articles/article_detail.asp?ArticleID=226

[66] Froomkin, Dan. "Affirmative Action Under Attack." *Washington Post,* October 1998 - http://www.washingtonpost.com/wp-srv/politics/special/affirm/affirm.htm. As on April 17, 2006.

[67] Fathers for Life (Walter H. Schneider) - http://www.fathersforlife.org/ussuic.htm. As in May 2004.

[68] McElroy, Wendy. "Are Fathers' Rights a Factor in Male Suicide?" *FOXNews.com,* January 29, 2002 -http://www.foxnews.com/story/0,2933,44183,00.html. As on April 17, 2006.

[69] Australian Institute of Health and Welfare (AIHW) media release, Male Suicides More Common than Road Deaths - http://www.aihw.gov.au/mediacentre/2000/mr20000711.html. As on April 17, 2006.

[70] Hoogland, Sharon & Randall Pieterse. *Suicide in Australia - A Dying Shame.* Wesley Mission, Sydney, Australia, November 2000 - http://www.wesleymission.org.au/publications/r&d/suicide.htm. As on April 17, 2006.

[71] Ibid.: /suicide.htm#causes.

[72] Arndt, Bettina. "Marginal Men." Sydney Morning Herald, October 10, 1998.

[73] McElroy, Wendy. "Are Fathers' Rights a Factor in Male Suicide?" *FOXNews.com.*

[74] Chesler, Phyllis. *Woman's Inhumanity to Woman.*

[75] Glick, Peter and Susan T. Fiske. "The Ambivalent Sexism Inventory: Differentiating Hostile and Benevolent Sexism." *Journal of Personality and Social Psychology, 70*(3) (1996): 491-512.

## NOTES TO CHAPTER 4 – THE MOST IMPORTANT EXPERIMENT EVER UNDERTAKEN

[1] Chateau Heartiste, 2012. Pope Paul VI On Birth Control Externalities: http://heartiste.wordpress.com/2012/12/02/pope-paul-vi-on-birth-control-externalities/

[2] Pope Paul VI, 1968. Humanae Vitae (On the Regulation of Human Births), Encyclical of Pope Paul VI: http://www.papalencyclicals.net/Paul06/p6humana.htm

[3] Bindel, J., 2012. In love with a death row dandy: http://www.newstatesman.com/lifestyle/lifestyle/2012/11/love-death-row-dandy

[4] Weininger, O., 1906. Sex and character. Translated from the 6th German edition ed. London, New York: London: William Heinemann. New York: G.P. Putnam's Sons.

## NOTES TO CHAPTER 5 – IT'S THE MATRIARCHY, STOOPID

[1] Diehm, J. (2013, December 10). 1 In 9 Girls Marries Before Age 15, And Here's What Happens To Them. *Huffington Post.* Retrieved December 10, 2013, from http://www.huffingtonpost.com/2013/12/05/child-marriage-_n_4393254.html

[2] Buchanan, M. (2013, December 12). Stephen Kamotho: A letter from Kenya. *A Voice for Men.* Retrieved Jan 17, 2014, from http://www.avoiceformen.com/misandry/stephen-kamotho-a-letter-from-kenya/

[3] Harford, T. (2006, February 18). I Do, I Do, I Do, I Do - The economic case for polygamy. *Slate.com.* Retrieved January 20, 2014, from http://www.slate.com/articles/arts/the_undercover_economist/2006/02/i_do_i_do_i_do_i_do.html

4 Polygyny. (2014, January 15). In Wikipedia, *The Free Encyclopedia*. Retrieved January 20, 2014, from http://en.wikipedia.org/wiki/Polygyny

5 Mehraspand, A. (2013, December 6). Indentured servitude for men in Iran: The myth of patriarchal oppressive divorce. *A Voice for Men*. Retrieved January 17, 2014, from http://www.avoiceformen.com/feminism/feminist-lies-feminism/indentured-servitude-for-men-in-iran-the-myth-of-patriarchal-oppressive-divorce/

6 World Health Organization. (2013, February). Female genital mutilation - Fact sheet N°241. Retrieved January 17, 2014, from http://www.who.int/mediacentre/factsheets/fs241/en/

7 Burrage, H. (2013, August 28). Fighting Female Genital Mutilation With Our Keyboards: The Feminist Statement on FGM Is Launched Today. *Huffington Post*. Retrieved January 17, 2014, from: http://www.huffingtonpost.co.uk/hilary-burrage/fighting-female-genital-mutilation_b_3822317.html

8 O'Hara, R. (2013, September 20). Circumcision in Africa not preventing HIV. *A Voice for Men*. Retrvd Jan 17, 2014 from: http://www.avoiceformen.com/updates/circumcision-in-africa-not-preventing-spread-of-hiv/

9 Relational aggression. (2013, November 14). In *Wikipedia, The Free Encyclopedia*. Retrieved January 17, 2014, from http://en.wikipedia.org/wiki/Relational_aggression

10 Chesler, P. (2009). *Woman's inhumanity to woman*. Lawrence Hill Books, 2009. Retrieved January 17, 2014, from http://www.phyllis-chesler.com/books/womans-inhumanity-to-woman

11 Complexity theory. (2013, October 28). In *Wikipedia, The Free Encyclopedia*. Retrieved January 20, 2014, from http://en.wikipedia.org/wiki/Complexity_theory

**NOTES TO CHAPTER 6 – EQUALITY WITH ESCAPE HATCH IS NOT EQUALITY**

1 Friedan, B. (1976). *It Changed My Life: Writings on the Women's Movement*. New York: Random House.

2 Cherry, K. (n.d.). Brain Plasticity:How Experience Changes the Brain. Retrvd July 18, 2015, from http://psychology.about.com/od/biopsychology/f/brain-plasticity.htm

3 Haier, R., Jung, R., Yeo, R., Head, K., & Alkire, M. (2005). The neuroanatomy of general intelligence: Sex matters. *NeuroImage*, *25*, 320-327.

4 Rationalization hamster. (2012, June 5). Urban Dictionary. Retrieved July 18, 2015, from: http://www.urbandictionary.com/define.php?term=rationalization+hamster

5 Neuroplasticity. (2014, January 9). In *Wikipedia, The Free Encyclopedia*. Retrieved January 17, 2014, from http://en.wikipedia.org/wiki/Neuroplasticity

6 Tieman, A. (2014, January 13). Men's Rights versus Feminism explained using magnets. *A Voice for Men*. Retrieved June 8, 2014, from http://www.youtube.com/watch?v=PF_WLlMWk6U

**NOTES TO CHAPTER 7 – ARE ALL WOMEN GOLD-DIGGERS?**

1 Breure, J. (Director). (2016, February 25). *Are All Men Pedophiles? Documentary* [Youtube – JW Productions]. Retrieved May 15, 2016, from https://youtu.be/GeiIBZkDy4o

[2] JW Productions. Are All Men Pedophiles? Documentary. (n.d.). Retrieved May 15, 2016, from http://areallmenpedophiles.com/

[3] Tomassi, R. (2016, May 6). Category Archives: Hypergamy. *The Rational Male*. Retrieved May 15, 2016, from http://therationalmale.com/category/hypergamy-2/

[4] Lunchboxcafe. (2013, November 28). *Black Friday - 2013 Wal Mart*. [Youtube]. Retrieved May 15, 2016, from http://youtu.be/ucrM3TLLJRs

[5] Bailey, J. (2011, November 25). *Black Friday Crowd Rushing into Urban Outfitters*. [Youtube]. Retrieved May 15, 2016, from http://youtu.be/DigiWS1YhxI

[6] kerry-washington.us. (2009, April 18). *L'Oreal – 'Because You're Worth It'*. [Youtube]. Retrieved May 15, 2016, from http://youtu.be/84SUfl8Yv4k

[7] Oliver, A. (2012, September 23). Imelda Marcos' famous collection of 3,000 shoes partly destroyed by termites and floods after lying in storage in the Philippines for 26 years since she exiled . *Daily Mail*. Retrieved May 15, 2016, from http://www.dailymail.co.uk/news/article-2207353/Imelda-Marcos-legendary-3-000-plus-shoe-collection-destroyed-termites-floods-neglect.html

[8] Unmasking Feminism. *Remove the Needs* (Repost from 2010). Retrieved January 19, 2014, from http://unmaskingfeminism.wordpress.com/2013/11/22/remove-the-needs-repost-from-2010/

[9] Oltermann, P. (2014, February 2). Female defence ministers pledge to break Europe's old boys' network. *The Guardian*. Retrieved May 13, 2016, from http://www.theguardian.com/world/2014/feb/02/female-defence-ministers-tweet-photograph

[10] Arndt, B. (2012, April 22). Why women lose the dating game. *The Sydney Morning Herald*. Retrieved May 16, 2016, from http://www.smh.com.au/lifestyle/life/why-women-lose-the-dating-game-20120421-1xdn0.html

[11] [11] Wex Legal Dictionary. (n.d.). Equal Protection. Retrieved May 15, 2016, from https://www.law.cornell.edu/wex/equal_protection

[12] Kassam, A. (2016, March 26). Canada urged to rethink approach to sexual assault after Ghomeshi acquittal. *The Guardian*. Retrieved May 15, 2016, from http://www.theguardian.com/world/2016/mar/26/canada-justice-system-ghomeshi-acquittal-sexual-assault-allegations-approach?utm_source=esp

[13] Franklin, R. (2014, January 21). Sara Ylen False Rape Claim Shows Ease With Which Innocent Men Convicted. *A Voice for Men*. Retrvd May 15, 2016, from http://www.avoiceformen.com/feminism/feminist-governance-feminism/sara-ylen-false-rape-claim-shows-ease-with-which-innocent-men-convicted/

[14] Davison, D. and J. Hembling. (2014, January 18). Canada: a first world cuntry. *A Voice for Men*. Retrieved May 15, 2016, from http://www.avoiceformen.com/gynarchy/canada-a-first-world-cuntry/

[15] Yeager, J. (2019, February 1). Hot Crazy Matrix A Man's Guide to Women - ORIGINAL. [Youtube]. Retrieved September 7, 2020, from https://youtu.be/pInk1rV2VEg

[16] Ibid.

**NOTES TO CHAPTER 8 – THE SUCCESS OF FEMINISM IS THE FAILURE OF SCIENCE**

[1] Galbi, Douglas (2015, September 11). Steven Pinker: sex, violence, and failure of enlightenment. *A Voice for Men*. Retrieved September 16, 2015, from http://www.avoiceformen.com/gynocentrism/steven-pinker-sex-violence-and-failure-of-enlightenment/

2 Zimmer, C., 2012. A Sharp Rise in Retractions Prompts Calls for Reform: http://www.nytimes.com/2012/04/17/science/rise-in-scientific-journal-retractions-prompts-calls-for-reform.html?pagewanted=all

3 Horton, R. (2015, April 11). Offline: What is medicine's 5 sigma? The Lancet, Vol 385 (9976), 1380. Retrieved July 20, 2015, from http://www.thelancet.com/pdfs/journals/lancet/PIIS0140-6736(15)60696-1.pdf

4 Binswanger, M. (2013, December 17). Excellence by Nonsense: The Competition for Publications in Modern Science (S. Bartling & S. Friesike, Eds.). Retrieved July 18, 2015, from Springer Link: http://link.springer.com/chapter/10.1007/978-3-319-00026-8_3/fulltext.html

## NOTES TO CHAPTER 9 – SPIRITUALITY, THE DOMAIN OF MEN

1 Coach Red Pill. (2020, August 11). *Treat a woman like a nerd*. Retrieved March 7, 2020, from Coach Red Pill [YouTube]: https://youtu.be/EGKpS1wVqL8

2 Diep, F. (2017, June 14). 8,000 years ago, 17 women reproduced for every one man. Retrieved January 31, 2021, from Pacific Standard: https://psmag.com/environment/17-to-1-reproductive-success

3 Karmin, M., Saag, L., Vicente, M., Wilson Sayres, M.A., Järve, M., Talas, U.G., et al (2015). A recent bottleneck of Y chromosome diversity coincides with a global change in culture. *Genome Research 25*(4), 459-466.

4 Baumeister, R. (2010). *Is there anything good about men?: How cultures flourish by exploiting men*. Oxford University Press.

5 Geggel, L. (2014). Humanity has more mothers than fathers, DNA reveals. LiveScience.com. Retrieved January 30, 2021, from: https://www.livescience.com/47976-more-mothers-in-human-history.html

6 Favre, M. & Sornette, D. (2011). Cooperation-male-female_Boston28June11. *ETH Zürich*. Retrieved January 30, 2021, from https://ethz.ch/content/dam/ethz/special-interest/mtec/chair-of-entrepreneurial-risks-dam/documents/Presentations/Cooperation_male_female_Boston28June11.pdf

7 Tomassi, R. (2020). *The RationalMale - Religion*. Reno, Nevada: Counterflow Media.

## NOTES TO CHAPTER 10 – CHOOSING YOUR RELIGION

1 Jarosek, S. (2013). Pragmatism, neural plasticity and mind-body unity. *Biosemiotics, 6*(2), 205-230. Retrieved from http://link.springer.com/article/10.1007%2Fs12304-012-9145-5

2 Jarosek, S. (2017). Quantum semiotics. Journal of Nonlocality: Special Issue on Psi and Nonlocal Mind, 5(1). http://journals.sfu.ca/jnonlocality/index.php/jnonlocality/article/view/64

3 Peirce, C. S. (1931–1935, & 1958). The collected papers of Charles Sanders Peirce. Vols. I–VI [C. Hartshorne & P. Weiss, Eds., 1931–1935], Vols. VII–VIII [A. W. Burks, Ed., 1958]. Cambridge, MA: Harvard University Press.

# INDEX

www.ingramcontent.com/pod-product-compliance
Lightning Source LLC
Chambersburg PA
CBHW072124020426
42334CB00018B/1700